Instant Shakespeare

Instant
Shakespeare

A PRACTICAL GUIDE FOR
ACTORS, DIRECTORS AND TEACHERS

Louis Fantasia

A & C Black

LONDON

First published 2002 by
Ivan R. Dee, Publisher,
1332 North Halsted Street, Chicago 60622, USA

This edition published 2004 by
A & C Black Publishers Limited
37 Soho Square, London W1D 3QZ

ISBN 0-7136-6853-9

A CIP catalogue record for this book is available from the British
Library

Printed and bound in the United States of America
by Quebecor World, Fairfield, Pennsylvania

Do your work, then step back . . .

We work with being, but nonbeing is what we use . . .

—Lao-tzu, *The Book of the Way*

Contents

Instant Shakespeare

Prelude:
Banging at Swords

WHEN IT COMES TO SHAKESPEARE, there are no experts. Not even me!

A quick look at the Shakespeare shelves in a library or bookstore shows you just how many people have opinions, backed by years of experience and scholarship, on just what a certain Shakespeare play means, or advice on how to act or direct Shakespeare. Often their advice and sets of rules conflict with one another.

I developed the Instant Shakespeare technique over twenty years of teaching and directing at the Shakespeare Globe Centre in London, and expanded and refined it in workshops and productions around the world. The workshops were designed so that actors, teachers, and directors with different levels of experience, working vocabularies, and cultures could come together quickly on the text itself without getting hung up on theory or terminology. The results really were instantaneous.

This book is therefore the result of my own, very personal Shakespearean odyssey. In it I have tried to balance my own experience teaching and directing Shakespeare with other techniques and approaches. I have also tried to encourage actors and directors to make *their* contributions and *their* choices, as long as these choices are informed by study, practice, and commitment.

It may seem strange, coming from the author of a Shakespeare book, to confess that I put off directing my first Shakespeare play for as long as I could. Reading Shakespeare had always put me to sleep. In college I flunked Shakespeare as an undergraduate, and have the transcripts to prove it. I avoided Shakespeare like the plague in graduate school. I was interested only in the modern theatre and in making films.

In the summer of 1975 I went to Paris directly from the American Film Institute, where I had studied filmmaking. I had written a silent film adaptation of Samuel Beckett's early short story "First Love." Alan Schneider, Beckett's great interpreter in the theatre, and Barney Rossett, his publisher at Grove Press, sent the script to Paris for Beckett's approval. My girlfriend was in Paris working on her doctorate in art history, so I went to France to spend some time with her and wait for Beckett. He finally sent the following telegram back to Barney Rossett:

DID NOT WRITE FIRST LOVE AS FILM. DO NOT WISH TO SEE FIRST LOVE AS FILM. LOVE, SAM.

So much for my film career. I decided to stay in France for the year and took a job as head of the theatre program at Schiller College, an American college in Strasbourg, near the German border. I set up a curriculum for the students, including the required Shakespeare courses, and created a season of plays which included works by George Tabori and Yukio Mishima, John Gay's *The Beggar's Opera,* a Goldoni comedy, and my own, very seventies adaptation of the Oedipus cycle of Sophocles. No Shakespeare.

One year turned into three. We developed a thriving theatre program. I was seeing the work of Brook, Mnouchkine, Strehler, Stein, and other Continental directors, which influenced me greatly, as did my friendship with Pierre Lefevre, a colleague of Michel St. Denis and one of the world's great acting teachers. I had the freedom to make all the mistakes I wanted, a very important opportunity in one's development. I could produce what I wanted, and I didn't have to direct any Shakespeare.

Or so I thought. One day the dean came to me and told me that the English community (mostly British diplomats and their wives) and the English-speaking friends of the school really wanted to see some Shakespeare in the theatre, and couldn't I please schedule some? He had been so good to me there, I couldn't say no. So I went to the library and pulled out the thinnest volume of Shakespeare I could find, *Macbeth*, and told him that is what we would do.

But I couldn't. Every time I began reading the play, I would either fall asleep or throw it down in disgust, thinking about those awful Witches, that stilted language. We worked on it in my acting classes, and I tried to sit in on the Shakespeare classes with my students, but I just couldn't do it.

In retrospect, I think my resistance to Shakespeare had something to do with the way in which it had been "fed" to me in school. Like Popeye's spinach, it was supposed to be good for me; it would make me a better person, smooth out my working-class edges, and all that. In other words, it would make me sound completely phony!

I was no fun to live with at that time, so I took myself to the movies one night to see Akira Kurosawa's *Throne of*

Blood, playing at the local French university cinema. This was Kurosawa's version of *Macbeth*, and I think it is one of the best film versions of Shakespeare ever made.

I returned inspired. I would direct the play as if it were a film project. I retyped the script (on an old manual portable typewriter) in screenplay format and decided to mount the production in and around the nineteenth-century French château that housed the college. I set the play in a World War I, Lafayette escadrille period. To me *Macbeth* was about personal honor more than ambition. The war in Vietnam had just ended, and World War I remained the last great "honorable" war—no concentration camps, no torture, just absurd charges of troops with fixed bayonets against machine guns, making the world safe for democracy.

We began rehearsals. The Witches were in trees for their first scene. Lady Macbeth was in a balcony watching the sun go down over the Rhine when she received Macbeth's letter. Duncan was murdered in the old stables off the château. Banquo was killed in a field, off in the distance. The audience would travel with the actors from scene to scene, through the magnificent old château and its grounds. The acting style was as realistic and cinematic as possible. We didn't move into the theatre until Act III, scene 4, when Macbeth became king and invited us to the banquet.

Now, this is really good, I thought, this is really moving along. Once inside the theatre (a converted stable), I was confident that the actors could keep the energy and reality going right through to the end of the play. You could hear the chopping down of trees outside the theatre as Birnam Wood approached.

But then came the swordfights! The fight master from the French National Theatre came to teach fencing. The kids loved it, and he did a great job, but I hated it! It looked so fake that I decided to avoid swordplay whenever possible. When Young Seward (in Act V) drew his saber and challenged Macbeth to fight, for instance, Macbeth smiled and instead took out his pistol and shot him before he could cross the stage. No honor there. And, to my relief, no swordfight either!

But we had the final combat between Macbeth and Macduff to deal with. The actor playing Macduff would bring the audience to tears in the scene when he received the news about his "chicks," and the fellow playing Macbeth would become increasingly demonic as the play progressed. They were headed for an ultimate conflict between good and evil, and now we appeared to be playing make-believe! I roughed up the fight choreography to make it look more realistic, and to allow the acting intentions to come through. But one of the actors was slightly hurt in rehearsal, and I could not take the chance of that happening in the heat of performance.

Then Nancy Amphoux, my students' wonderfully intimidating Shakespeare teacher, told me of an essay she had once read which included the phrase "banging at swords." The phrase stuck in her memory—and in mine—because it addressed a fundamental issue of staging Shakespeare.

In a production you work to make the language real, the setting real, the interpretation real. Then all reality abruptly stops as you "bang" at make-believe swordplay. Since most of the swordfights in Shakespeare occur near the end of the plays, dramatic intensity often wanes, and the play stumbles to its end instead of culminating grandly in the physical release of energy. The same is true in the comedies, where the dances and masques are so crucial.

Nancy went on to give other examples of "banging at swords" in Shakespeare: the storm in *King Lear*, Juliet's suicide, the hoisting up of Antony to Cleopatra in the monument. In all these instances, unless you're very careful, you can look quite ridiculous in your staging, or you may be forced to take a position of agreed-upon make-believe with the audience (with everyone saying, in effect, "It's only Shakespeare!").

Nancy wasn't looking for more or better special effects. Rather, she was suggesting to me a more theatrical kind of thinking. If I couldn't solve the "banging at swords" scenes in my production, then I probably hadn't solved the real issues of the play.

Well, there it was, a challenge from a scholar. I didn't want the actors to get hurt, and I didn't want the play to end with a whimper. So what could I do? How would I stop "banging at swords"?

We traded the safe fencing foils for genuine World War I cavalry sabers. In a rehearsal with the two actors and myself, we worked it out. At close range they would make one, two, three passes at full strength, sparks flashing from their swords. On the fourth pass, Macbeth went for Macduff's head; Macduff ducked and the blade stuck in the beam of the theatre. In the performances you heard the audience gasp when they realized that these swords were real and that these guys weren't kidding.

From that moment on, an interesting thing happened. The element of danger had been planted in the audience's mind. (Remember, drama is expectation mixed with uncertainty.) The actors returned immediately to their safe combat choreography, but now the audience supplied the danger. When the fight spilled out into the muddy road behind the theatre (an homage to Kurosawa, who always includes a battle in the rain in his films), the audience rushed out to follow the action to its bloody end.

No "banging at swords" here, thank goodness! The only

better swordfight I've seen on stage was in Stephen Berkoff's modern-dress version of *Hamlet*. Here Hamlet and Laertes went at it without swords, instead pointing their index fingers accusingly at each other, as children do on a playground. The *sound* that the actors made as they fought—"whoosh-whoosh, swish-swish"—electrified the scene and allowed them to fight and to act at a pace that would have been impossibly dangerous had they actually used weapons. That's how my odyssey with Shakespeare began, "banging at swords."

Introduction:
The Absence of Presence

SINCE THOSE STRASBOURG DAYS nearly three decades ago, I have traveled the globe directing and teaching Shakespeare, giving workshops and lectures, often on behalf of the Shakespeare Globe Centre. Everything I knew about Shakespeare was written on two worn index cards that traveled with me. The first card had two columns:

Nouns	I. About
Verbs	II. Tune
I/thou	III. Texture
adj./adv.	IV. End
rep. for breath	

... and a line of code—"u-/u-/u-/u-/u-/"—at the bottom, while the second card said:

why, etc.??

followed by a long squiggly line, and below that:

order/disorder/rebellion—yes? no?—2nd order.

That was it. That was Instant Shakespeare!

From those cards I could deliver a thirty-minute lecture, a two-day workshop, or a six-week class, depending on the audience, its level of experience, talent, and the depth it wanted to explore. A second major consideration was whether the workshop was geared to teachers, students, actors, directors, or the general public. The information was the same, but the level of intensity and expectation varied.

People in my workshops and classes often asked me when I was going to write my book. I would reply, half jokingly, "How can I write a book when everything I know is on the back of two index cards?" What I was really afraid of was my missing presence.

I believe that knowledge, growth, and understanding can come only through presence—the contact that comes from being there. Will you understand what was on those cards if you and I are not in the same room, experiencing the same process at the same time? I hope so.

I've structured this book to give you as much of an idea of my presence as possible: who I am, what I have to say, and why I think it is important to say it. At the same time I have allowed room, as I do in my workshops, for your own presence and development through exercises and assignments, periods of reflection, rethinking, and reevaluation. Most important, I've allowed time for confusion.

It is essential that you put this book down from time to time in order to complete the exercises and let them sink in. Too few people understand that creativity emerges out of chaos and that confusion is a prerequisite to growth and knowledge. Art is made by living with hard and difficult questions over a long period of time.

This book will raise more questions than it answers. If that doesn't interest you, stop now. There are plenty of Shakespeare "cookbooks" with "instant" recipes for monologues, characters, term papers, and scenes. Perhaps this is why most of the Shakespeare we see on stage and in class is so dull and boring—actors make superficial decisions about complex characters and are not fully present in their work.

Instant Shakespeare is not this kind of cookbook, nor is it a collection of audition monologues or study guides, although there are many quick fixes, outlines, and soliloquies included here. *Instant Shakespeare* is an old-fashioned "grammar," a set of ground rules to help you get under the surface of the verse, the line, the scene, under the skin of the character and beneath what I later call the "sand" of a performance. It is "instant" because anyone can do the basic work without resorting to scholarly research or years of drama training.

I considered opening this book with theoretical information, but that would contradict what I believe is the true, creative method of learning: experience first, followed by questioning, reflection, and, with luck, inspiration. Of course, you can always cheat and go to the end, but I hope you won't.

Within these pages I've included all the primary materials that you need. Occasionally I refer to scenes or to complete plays, so, while not essential, a complete works of Shakespeare or a collection of the individual plays is helpful.

A book, like a workshop, an accident on the street, or a theatrical performance, is an example of an *encounter*, where we meet as strangers and hope to be understood. As I stand at the threshold of this encounter, I undertake the responsibility for saying something truly worthwhile about Shakespeare. Ernest Becker once wrote, "The most any of us can seem to do is to fashion something—an object or ourselves—and drop it into the confusion, make an offering of it . . . to the life force." This book, then, is my offering.

PART ONE

Pre-Performance— Instant Shakespeare!

To be or not to be, that is the question. . . .

There! You've said it. Instant Shakespeare!

Say everything in **bold** aloud. **Be bold.** (Did you say that?)

It's the only way I know to begin building up your "voice." Once again, if you didn't say those famous, intimidating, overused "Shakespearean" words, then **be bold** and go back and say them now:

To be or not to be, that is the question. . . .

There, that wasn't so hard, was it?

The reading you have just done is an act of pre-performance.

One of the things I hope you'll get from *Instant Shakespeare* is the confidence to trust your instincts and to find your own voice in Shakespeare. We all read with a voice, either the silent one in our head or the spoken one in performance. Whichever voice we use, it must be developed when reading a play, particularly a play by Shakespeare, so that we read with a growing understanding of a play's three-dimensional nature.

The reading of a play differs from the reading of a novel, poem, or short story because a play's text implies performance. A play's text hints of previous interpretations and implies future ones. We read a play to discover how it might have been or might be performed. It is a blueprint for performance.

A play, therefore, is a two-dimensional implication of a past or future three-dimensional event. Reading a play as a blueprint for performance requires you to engage in four levels of discovery. These four levels are basic, like the four food groups, and no play can be truly read without going through each of them. They are:

1. Know what the individual words really mean (dialogue).
2. Know where the play is going (structure).
3. Know the rhythm and sense of the line (character).
4. Know what the play is about (the central event).

The first section of this book gives you the tools and techniques needed to acquire these four levels of knowledge. The second section teaches you how to apply them to performance. In other words, the first part of *Instant Shakespeare* is about analysis; the second is about interpretation.

Each of us, whether we are actors, directors, teachers, students, or theatregoers, has the ability to give voice to our readings through analysis and interpretation. This is true whether we choose to do it privately in our heads or publicly on stage. The richer the voice of the reader, the richer the reading of the text. The richer the reading of the text, the richer the experience of the play. The richer the play, the richer our lives will be for our encounter with Shakespeare and his theatre. This is one of the goals of *Instant Shakespeare*.

· 1 ·

Know What the Words
Really Mean—Dialogue

LET'S START WITH finding out what Shakespeare's words really mean—not by looking them up in a dictionary (or worse, in the notes on the bottom of the page) but in a three-dimensional, "instant" way.

The Shakespeare Paradigm

The Shakespeare Paradigm is the question you apply to every line and every word of every Shakespeare play. Answering it enables you to proceed to the next word, line, or scene with intelligence and confidence. The Shakespeare Paradigm is this:

> Why does this particular character say these particular words, in this particular order, at this particular moment?

This is the "why, etc.?" of my original 3 x 5 index card, and I shall refer to it throughout *Instant Shakespeare*. The answer you give to this question will drive your particular reading of the text, either in the classroom or in performance, by providing a specific, playable, and produceable meaning.

What is the difference between a character who says, "So *foul* and fair a day I have not seen . . ." (as Macbeth does) and one who says, "So *fair* and foul a day I have not seen . . ."? What is the difference between a character who says (as Hamlet does), "Oh, what a rogue and peasant slave *am I* . . ." and one who says, "Oh, what a rogue and peasant slave *I am* . . ."?

The words are the same, the meter is the same, but something is different beyond the mere transposition of words. Let's find out what.

Frog Overlays

In the old days, before computers and the Internet, students studied biology from books with plastic overlays of frogs in them, one overlay for each of the systems in the anatomy—skeletal, circulatory, nervous, digestive, and so on. With these overlays you could study each of the frog's systems individually. Then, when you put them together, one on top of the other, you got a good picture of a dissected frog.

In this pre-performance section we will examine plays in the same way—as "dead" texts, primed for autopsy, whose systems we will study individually. A dead play, for me, is a play that is not yet living and breathing on stage. It is my belief that you can breathe life back into a text only after you've done a thorough analysis of it. So let's begin.

These are the "frog overlays" of *Instant Shakespeare*:

1. Make the nouns sound like what they mean.
2. Push the verbs.
3. Leave the adjectives and adverbs alone.
4. Play the "I/thou" and "I/it" relationships.
5. Repunctuate for breath.

OVERLAY 1. MAKE THE NOUNS SOUND LIKE WHAT THEY
MEAN

Oh, what a **rogue** and peasant **slave** am I.

What do you see in your mind's eye when you say the
words "rogue" and "slave"?

For the moment, let's assume there is no right or wrong
answer; what you see may be completely different from what
I see, and this is what will make our interpretations unique.
The important thing is to have a specific and concrete impulse that produces each image, each word. It is what T. S
Eliot called the "objective correlative"—the real object that
the language attempts to bring forth and re-create.

In other words, what is the specific image of a rogue and
a slave you want the listener to see? Let me clarify this with
two other examples (all **nouns** are in **bold**):

MACBETH: Is this a **dagger** which I see before me,
The **handle** toward my **hand**? Come, let me clutch thee!

JULIET: Gallop apace, you fiery-footed **steeds**,
Towards Phoebus' **lodging**; such a **wagoner**
As **Phaeton** would whip you to the west
And bring in cloudy **night** immediately.

Why does Macbeth choose to say "dagger" and not
"hatchet," "stiletto," "penknife," or "broadsword" at that
moment? Shakespeare could easily have given him another
word to say. Why is "dagger" the only noun Macbeth can
use to describe what he sees?

Why does Juliet choose to say "steeds" and not "horses,"
"ponies," "nags," or "mules"? She could, but instead she
chooses "steeds"—the only noun she can use to describe exactly what she sees.

We don't say things in the theatre just because the play-wright put them there. Each word, each image must have an *impulse*, a motivation, and a reason for existence. Providing this impulse is relatively simple with daggers, steeds, rogues, and peasant slaves. It becomes more complicated, however, when we talk about abstractions: "the quality of mercy," "outrageous fortune," or "justice, justice, justice, justice."

Invariably at this point, one of my students asks, "You don't really want me to 'do' it this way, do you?" If by "do" you mean perform, the answer is no; this is not even a re-hearsal technique, let alone a performance technique. It is a tool for analysis, for pre-performance autopsy. But, yes, I want you to say it this way, **out loud,** as you begin work on the texts. That said, let's continue.

OVERLAY 2. PUSH THE VERBS
Verbs are action words. Push them. In this line it's easy:

Oh, what a rogue and peasant slave **am** I.

Do you suspect that the verb "to be" occupies a special place in *Hamlet*? Let's return to our other two examples (all **verbs** are in **bold** now):

JULIET: **Gallop** apace, [she makes those horses move!] you
   fiery-footed steeds,
   Towards Phoebus' lodging; such a wagoner
   As Phaeton would **whip** you to the west
   And **bring** in cloudy night immediately.
   Spread thy close curtain, love-performing night,
   That runaways' eyes may **wink** and Romeo
   Leap to these arms, untalk'd of and unseen. . . .

MACBETH: **Is** this a dagger which I **see** before me,
   The handle toward my hand? **Come,** let me **clutch** thee!

I **have** thee not and yet I **see** thee still.
Art thou not, fatal vision, sensible
To feeling as to sight, or **art** thou but
A dagger of the mind, a false creation
Proceeding from the heat-oppressed brain?

Notice that this makes the monologues move more quickly. One of the things we're working toward is the sense of a longer breath supporting a longer line. This results in a longer thought. You don't think word by word; why should you act word by word? (It also makes the monologues easier to memorize, but more of that anon!)

Remember, verbs are action words. Plays are about actions. Push the verbs and you will push the play forward! Putting the two overlays together gives you something like this (**be bold, now**):

MACBETH: **Is** this a **dagger** which I **see** before me,
The **handle** toward my **hand**? **Come**, let me **clutch** thee!
I **have** thee not and yet I **see** thee still.
Art thou not, fatal **vision**, sensible
To **feeling** as to **sight**, or **art** thou but
A **dagger** of the **mind**, a false **creation**
Proceeding from the heat-oppressed **brain**?

JULIET: **Gallop** apace, you fiery-footed **steeds**,
Towards Phoebus' **lodging**; such a **wagoner**
As **Phaeton** would **whip** you to the **west**
And **bring** in cloudy **night** immediately.
Spread thy close **curtain**, love-performing **night**,
That runaways' **eyes** may **wink** and **Romeo**
Leap to these **arms**, untalk'd of and unseen.

Now the monologues begin to stand on their own in a three-dimensional way, allowing us to see the principal images—the sun traveling east to west, the dagger in the air, and night coming on.

OVERLAY 3. LEAVE THE ADJECTIVES AND ADVERBS ALONE

Oh, what a rogue and **peasant** slave am I.

There's no need to gild the lily! Shakespeare was quite capable of embellishing his own images. What you need to do is to tell the story. Play the action, not the poetry.

Take the famous typing test sentence, for example: *The quick brown fox jumps over the lazy dog.*

Which makes more sense to you: *The quick brown over the lazy* or *Fox jumps dog?* It's a headline, isn't it? Fox jumps dog, film at eleven! We want to know more about the fox and dog—what they are like, what they were doing, what their relationship is. The same is true in the theatre—especially in the theatre!

An audience wants to know what's going on, what happens next, and who will do what to whom, when, and why. When you stress the adjectives and adverbs, especially in Shakespeare, the audience drops out. They know *you* must be having a jolly good time up there, because you're acting away at your Shakespeare, but they feel left out because they are not engaged in the story you are telling. They are, at best, mesmerized by the sound of your voice, but more often are numbed by meaningless language.

Here is Juliet's speech again, this time stressing the adjectives and adverbs:

Gallop **apace**, you **fiery-footed** steeds,
Towards **Phoebus'** lodging; such a wagoner
As Phaeton would whip you to the west
And bring in **cloudy** night **immediately**.
Spread thy **close** curtain, **love-performing** night,

That **runaways'** eyes may wink and Romeo
Leap to these arms, **untalk'd** of and **unseen.**

Read it out loud. Do you see what's happening? The seductive and dangerous thing is to play the adverbs and adjectives in order to make the text sound more "Shakespearean"
(**peasant** slaves and **fiery-footed** steeds and **solid** flesh). It's
great fun to do BAAAD SHAKESPEARE, but it makes little sense
to an audience.

And that, in a simple, direct, and immediate way, is what
we want to avoid. At the bare minimum, a theatrical event,
especially a Shakespearean event, should make sense! Theatre is an act of communication, not an evening of beautiful,
meaningless sounds—"Muzak" or "wallpaper" Shakespeare
rolling on forever. It's easy to listen to but is ultimately meaningless to the audience. We've all had the experience of sitting in the theatre and watching someone act Shakespeare,
our minds floating off to the grocery list, the baby-sitter, or
what we want for dinner. If this is Shakespeare, then please,
just put me out of my misery!

OVERLAY 4. PLAY THE "I/THOU" AND "I/IT"
RELATIONSHIPS
"I/Thou" and "I/It" describe concepts of the theologian Martin Buber (1878–1965), one of the great religious philoso-
phers of the twentieth century. Buber's thinking had a great
impact on both modern theology and the human potential
movement of the past thirty years. He believed that an eter-
nal Thou, a divine presence, can be glimpsed in every particular Thou.

Later, in Chapter 15, we will explore this idea of presence
and its meaning for the work we do in the theatre. But for
now we will employ Buber's terms in their most literal sense:
whom are you talking to and what are you talking about? Is

the meaning of each and every line so clear that everyone, on stage and off, knows exactly whom you are talking to and what you are talking about?

"I/Thou" expresses mutuality and recognition between persons (you and me—I must *see* you before I can name you) while "I/It" expresses functional behavior (me and it—the object in its relationship to me). "I/Thou" assumes an encounter, a relationship between persons based on mutual giving and listening.

Oh, what a rogue and peasant slave am I.

Whom is the speaker addressing, himself or the audience? Is he talking about himself or another character? Does he shift? Why?

You must have a "partner" on each and every line you deliver—a connection, a relationship, with someone or something (the "thou" or the "it") to give the line its reason for being. Any moment when you're unaware of your thou/it partner, the audience will know and immediately check out. STOP! Reconnect!

In Shakespeare, partnering is essential and simple. Shakespeare's characters speak to one another, themselves, the audience, or God. That's it. A simple litmus test of trial and error will help you get to the truth—your own truth of who or what your partner is at that particular moment.

Suppose your Hamlet delivers the "peasant rogue" lines to himself. If that doesn't seem to work, then shift gears and change to another reading. He delivers them full out to the audience. Or to God in exasperation! (We already know he doesn't say them to the other actor, the Player, on stage behind him.) It will cost you nothing but a little time to test it out.

It is necessary to say here that while there is no right or wrong way at this stage in your work, it is important to commit to one decision at a time. Try it out fully and completely. If it doesn't work, change it. If you play everything at once, you get mushy ambiguity! **Be bold** . . . but be specific!

Let's look at Macbeth. When does he speak *to* the dagger and when does he speak *about* it? There are no absolutes here, no rights or wrongs, but you'll notice that the "I/thou" relationships have a great deal to do with where you breathe in the text:

MACBETH: Is **this** a dagger which I see before me,
   The handle toward my hand?

Of whom is he asking the question? Himself, the audience, God, or the dagger?

   Come, let me clutch **thee**! [You, the dagger]

The next line implies a stage direction that Macbeth clutch for the dagger and miss:

   I have **thee** not and yet I see **thee** still.

In the next four lines, is he talking *to* the dagger or *about* the dagger? To himself or us?

   Art **thou** not, fatal vision, sensible
   To feeling as to sight, or art **thou** but
   A dagger of the mind, a false creation
   Proceeding from [it] the heat-oppressed brain?

And now where is reality?

   I see **thee** yet, in form as palpable
   As **this** which now I draw. . . .

Once you become accustomed to doing it, this "thou/it" partnering will give your work great clarity and precision. Trust me.

OVERLAY 5. REPUNCTUATE FOR BREATH

Modern editions of Shakespeare's plays are generally over-punctuated. If you examine the Quarto editions (pirated copies published during Shakespeare's lifetime) and the First Folio (published just after his death) you'll notice that punctuation and spelling are used with greater informality than is the case today. The important thing to understand here is that, whichever edition you're using, the punctuation will greatly affect your reading of the play. Let me give you a simple example from *Antony and Cleopatra*:

Though the two have been rivals, when Caesar Augustus hears the news of Marc Antony's death, he says (unpunctuated):

> Look you sad friends
> The gods rebuke me but it is (a) tidings
> To wash the eyes of kings.

The First Folio (1623) leaves out the "a" and punctuates it as follows:

> Look you sad friends,
> The gods rebuke me, but it is tidings
> To wash the eyes of kings.

The Third Folio (1663) prints it this way:

> Look you, sad friends,
> The gods rebuke me, but it is a tidings
> To wash the eyes of kings.

The Arden edition (1981) has it this way:

> Look you sad, friends?
> The gods rebuke me, but it is a tidings
> To wash the eyes of kings.

Do you see how the punctuation changes the meaning of the line? One of the reasons I prefer the Arden edition, even though I sometimes disagree with its editors, is its practice of printing alternative readings in the notes at the bottom of each page. This way I can see several options and make up my own mind.

You can spend years studying Elizabethan punctuation, but *Instant Shakespeare* gives you a shortcut.

First, photocopy the text. Then, take some liquid correction fluid and white out all the punctuation. That's right, all of it!

Now, reading aloud, work through the nouns and verbs, leave the adjectives and adverbs alone, play the "I/thou" and "I/it" relationships, and punctuate only when and where you need to breathe. For the moment, don't worry whether the punctuation mark should be a comma, semicolon, or period. Just ask yourself if you need a long pause, a short pause, or no pause for sense, meaning, and breath.

> Oh [,] what a rogue and peasant slave am I [.]

The comma, at that point in the sentence, encourages you to pause, to sigh, to self-indulge. Very thespy, very Shakespearean, and very boring. Worse still, some editions use an exclamation point—Oh!

Not only can punctuation profoundly change the meaning of a text, it can even alter the staging of the line and the entire event on stage. Take, for example, the opening lines of *Twelfth Night*, one of Shakespeare's best-known speeches:

If music be the food of love, play on,
Give me excess of it that, surfeiting,
The appetite may sicken and so die.
That strain again, it had a dying fall.
                              —Oxford Edition

If music be the food of love, play on;
Give me excess of it; that surfeiting,
The appetite may sicken, and so die.—
That strain again; it had a dying fall:
                              —Globe Edition

If music be the food of love, play on,
Give me excess of it, that, surfeiting
The appetite may sicken, and so die.
That strain again; it had a dying fall:
                              —Arden Edition

See how the differences in punctuation change the implied stage action? When is the music playing? When does it stop? Does the lovesick Duke speaking these lines stop it? When does the music start up again? Does he stop and sigh with every pause? Does he rush around madly? All of this is indicated or implied by the punctuation.

To put it simply, whose instincts, whose "voice" are you going to follow, yours or the editor's? Now, take those four lines and repunctuate only for breath:

If music be the food of love play on
Give me excess of it that surfeiting
The appetite may sicken and so die
That strain again it had a dying fall

These are by no means the only options, but when I do this exercise I get a strong first line, almost a command, up to "play on"; then a long second sentence going from "Give me excess" to "die"; then a long pause while the speaker waits and listens as the music begins again; and finally, as he hears the dying fall, "That strain again."

The point is that you, the reader, and not the editor, decide what the text says and how it is said! *There are no experts.*

Let's look once more at Juliet's speech and pause at the punctuation marks the editors have inserted. Use a short pause for commas, longer for semicolons, and longer still for the colons.

> **Gallop apace, [*pause*] you fiery-footed steeds, [*pause*]**
> **Towards Phoebus' lodging; [*long pause*] such a wagoner**
> **As Phaeton would whip you to the west [*pause*]**
> **And bring in cloudy night immediately.**

You can feel the life go out of the speech like air out of a tire! Now remove the punctuation and pause only when you need to take a breath. Remember, this isn't a contest to see who can stay underwater longest!

> **Gallop apace you fiery-footed steeds**
> **Towards Phoebus' lodging such a wagoner**
> **As Phaeton would whip you to the west**
> **And bring in cloudy night immediately.**

Which one sounds more like an eager teenager? Now we are beginning to make thinking synonymous with breathing, a kind of "idea-breathing," which is how we begin the transition from dead texts to living ones, from analysis to performance. You must quite literally breathe life into these texts in order to perform them. Once you trust yourself to breathe as you think, your reading will take on enormous energy and dynamism.

The Shakespeare Paradigm Revisited

Now that we have acquired a method for getting beneath the surface of Shakespeare's verse, let's return to the Shakespeare Paradigm: Why does this particular character say these particular words, in this particular order, at this particular moment?

One of the first things I ask students and actors to do is to copy out a text—by hand if you're really serious, but photocopying will do. Then, take a black marker and blot out the "thespy" words. The "thespy" words (as in thespian, from Thespis, the first actor) are the ones that sound funny, actory, or old-fashioned. You might be embarrassed to use them in contemporary, colloquial speech. They sound good, but you really don't understand them. In short, they are "Shakespearean." Take another look at Hamlet's "peasant slave" monologue:

> Oh, what a rogue and peasant slave am I.
> Is it not monstrous that this player here,
> But in a fiction, in a dream of passion,
> Could force his soul so to its own conceit
> That from her working all his visage waned,
> Tears in his eyes, distraction in his aspect,
> A broken voice, and his whole function suiting
> With forms to his conceit? And all for nothing!
> For Hecuba!

If I delete the words that seem "thespy" to me, the speech sounds like this:

> Oh, what a . . . slave am I. Is it not monstrous
> that this player . . . in a fiction, in a
> dream of passion, Could force his soul so . . .
> That . . . Tears in his eyes . . . A broken voice . . .
> And all for nothing! . . .

Nothing too painful there, is there? And the speech still seems to make some sort of sense. The speaker is saying that he feels inadequate because an actor can manufacture make-believe emotions while he cannot experience genuine ones. We don't yet know why this is (insanity, melancholy, self-awareness, or what), but before we can find out, we must analyze. If you know the play, try to forget it for the moment. Concentrate on just this fragment now, and refill the blanks. Put the thespy words back in, one at a time, asking yourself each time *why* this character needs to say *this* particular word, at *this* particular moment, in *this* particular order. Look again at Hamlet's very first line:

Oh, what a rogue and peasant slave am I.

Why does this character choose to say *rogue* (rogue elephant?) and not "bum"? Why *peasant* slave, as opposed to "dirty slave"? What does the speaker actually mean by using those particular words and not others?

As you go through each line, filling in the blanks:

1. Make the nouns sound like what they mean.
2. Push the verbs.
3. Leave the adjectives and adverbs alone.

For the moment we don't need to worry about playing the "I/thou" relationships or repunctuating for breath. We are about to go "running for our Onions"!

Rats and Onions

C. T. Onions was an editor of the *Oxford English Dictionary* who catalogued all the words in the *OED* that turned up in Shakespeare. He published them in a book entitled *A Shakespeare Glossary* (1986), a handy little volume that tells you what the words meant when Shakespeare first used them. I keep a copy beside me at all times in rehearsal and use it for backup whenever I "smell a rat."

Smelling a rat is what happens when you are paying close attention to the words, and the words you're hearing or speaking don't make any sense; they've become wallpaper Shakespeare or iambic pentameter Muzak.

For example, at a workshop of mine in Tokyo, a few of the actors asked me to take a look at a scene from *Richard II*. They said something was wrong. It was the scene in Act III in which the Gardener speaks of the pending overthrow of the King:

> Depressed he is already, and deposed
> 'Tis doubt he will be. Letters came last night
> To a dear friend of the good Duke of York's
> That tell black tidings.

They were right. There was something wrong with the scene. Any ideas? Can you smell the rat? Don't worry, it took me a few passes at it before I went running for my Onions! I'll play the *Jeopardy* theme while you try and figure it out.

Time's up. The rat is "depressed"!

In the Elizabethan era the word "depressed" did not have the psychological connotations it has today. According to Onions, it meant "humbled" or "reduced in rank," not moody or sad. By playing the modern meaning of the word, the Gardener was unduly sympathetic toward Richard and thus tilted the emotional weight of the scene in the wrong direction.

Another "rat" appears early in *Hamlet*, when the Ghost first appears, and says that he must "render up" himself to tormenting flames. Not only does "render" mean surrender or give up (to "Caesar the things that are Caesar's," for example), but it also means burn away, or reduce (as you might with fat or butter in the kitchen). This second meaning clearly connects the speech to the melting of "solid" flesh into a dew later in the play.

Remember, this is all a part of our first basic system, knowing what the words really mean.

Bag and Baggage

We must know what Shakespeare's words mean, and then communicate that meaning to the audience and to our students. This may seem obvious, but it's our biggest challenge in performing or teaching Shakespeare.

Not knowing what the words mean is what makes our eyes glaze over when we read the plays. Not knowing puts an audience to sleep when we perform. The problem most people have with "Shakespeare" isn't really Shakespeare's fault. He never meant to terrorize, intimidate, or bore anyone with his writing. He was, by all accounts, a successful playwright. So why are people so adversely affected when they open up one of his plays?

It's the "baggage"—the very weight of Shakespeare's reputation as the greatest writer in the English language—that gets in our way. He is a "genius," "unique," "royal."

We each have our impression of Shakespeare, the one we received from a high school teacher, our first visit to the theatre, or watching *Hamlet* on film. Even before we read or see the plays, we seem to know, in a foggy pre-Freudian, post-Jungian part of our brain, that Hamlet is a melancholy Dane dressed in black, that there are three witches in *Macbeth*, and that Shylock is a moneylending Jew.

And this experience, whether from school or the theatre, leads us to believe that we need guides, experts, editors, and footnotes to help us through the plays, because—heaven help us—we can never read them on our own, let alone understand them.

Nonsense, I say! Shakespeare's plays are written in a version of English that is only four hundred years old; English after Shakespeare didn't so much change as become more simple. It is not as rich now as it was when Shakespeare was writing and creating a new language from Old English, Norman French, and Latin. We may find Shakespeare's language occasionally difficult, ornate, or obscure, but not as often as we think. On average, in all the workshops I've done, my students have difficulty with only 10 to 15 percent of Shakespeare's vocabulary. Even so, in classwork, workshops, and rehearsals, I repeatedly discover people saying words out loud without knowing what they mean. We excuse this because we think we know how to "do" Shakespeare.

"Doing" Shakespeare

One of my pet peeves is being told by students or teachers that they don't know how to "do" Shakespeare, or worse, that they've "done" lots of Shakespeare. This "doing" of Shakespeare is one of the most frightening phrases I know. It's like "doing" macramé or jail time! It usually means that the actors have learned to shift into a "classical" mode, doing things with their voices, bodies, and psyches that they would never think of doing with, or to, any other playwright.

Similarly, I have seen perfectly capable and dedicated teachers withdraw in pain and terror when it comes time to teach the Shakespeare "unit." They will show films of the plays, especially *Romeo and Juliet, Hamlet,* and *Macbeth,* then proceed with complicated lesson plans about Renaissance cooking, dancing, swordfights, and mask making—

anything to avoid actually having to read the play and say the words!

One of the mistakes we make in theatre is that of "just doing it," as if analysis and technique were anathema to creativity. We often do too much too soon, making choices with insufficient information too early in the creative process. Actors and directors will spend four or five weeks in rehearsal, only to have the direction of the project change entirely in the last few days before opening night, because the truth of "what the play was about" suddenly emerged. This is, at the very least, a terribly inefficient way of working.

In drama schools and acting classes, Shakespeare is usually handled as something "other," for which one must receive specialized preparation. Students are trained, depending on the methods of their teachers, to work on the self, the voice, or the body through personal, emotional, and situational exercises. Text work and scene study are geared toward establishing comfortable and honest emotional and psychological connections to the material, rather than coming to grips with its structural demands.

None of this is very satisfying, and the results are usually pretty embarrassing! If you get nothing else from *Instant Shakespeare*, learn to do your homework. Know what the words really mean!

Chapter Exercise

If you've performed the exercises so far, you should begin to see the monologues "stand up," in a three-dimensional way. Here is a speech of Oberon's from *A Midsummer Night's Dream*. Go through it with your "frog overlays," continually posing the Shakespeare Paradigm. You will not be able to fully answer these questions without reading the entire play,

but for now, just knowing what the words really mean will
be enough.

> I know a bank where the wild thyme blows,
> Where oxlips and the nodding violet grows,
> Quite overcanopied with luscious woodbine,
> With sweet musk-roses, and with eglantine.
> There sleeps Titania sometime of the night,
> Lulled in these flowers with dances and delight;
> And there the snake throws her enamelled skin
> Weed wide enough to wrap a fairy in;
> And with the juice of this I'll streak her eyes,
> And make her full of hateful fantasies.
> Take thou some of it and seek through this grove:
> A sweet Athenian lady is in love
> With a disdainful youth. Anoint his eyes,
> But do it when the next thing he espies
> May be the lady. Thou shalt know the man
> By the Athenian garments he hath on.
> Effect it with some care, that he may prove
> More fond on her than she upon her love;
> And look thou meet me ere the first cock crow.

· 2 ·

The Histrionic
Sensibility

THINK YOU REALLY KNOW what the words mean and why this particular character says these particular words at this particular moment in this particular order? Good. Then let me ask you this again:

What's the difference between a character who says:

Oh, what a rogue and peasant slave **am I**

. . . and one who says:

Oh, what a rogue and peasant slave **I am**?

Between one who says:

So **foul and fair** a day I have not seen

. . . and one who says:

So **fair and foul** a day I have not seen?

On the surface, the statements are identical except for the order of two words. If we were to paraphrase the lines, we would come up with about the same "meaning." And if we were to translate both sets of lines into another language, the translations would be about the same. Perhaps Shakespeare was running out of ink, candles, or moonlight; or was hung over or had a hot date and really couldn't be bothered to tell you if he meant I am, or am I, foul or fair, fair or foul, and don't be so picky anyway, dear boy!

But the position of these little monosyllables indicates and alters the essence of the speaker's character. Remember, at this point in the plays we don't yet know anything about Macbeth or Hamlet. Never heard of them. All we have is this particular fragment to go on.

You won't be able to solve this puzzle by running to your Onions or checking the footnotes or searching the Shakespeare home page on the Internet. You can solve it only by saying the words aloud:

> **So foul and fair a day I have not seen**
> **So fair and foul a day I have not seen;**

and

> **Oh, what a rogue and peasant slave am I**
> **Oh, what a rogue and peasant slave I am.**

Macbeth first. In which reading is the glass half empty, and in which is the glass half full? Which speaker sees the potential for evil in the world, and which the potential for goodness?

The Hamlet of the "am I" line sounds reflective, self-aware, and inward-looking. He has looked deep inside himself and doesn't like what he finds. It is the sadder of the two readings.

The Hamlet of the "I am" line, on the other hand, sounds pleased with himself, smug—a self-satisfied grin is implied at the end of the line. This speaker has more in common with Richard III or Iago than with Hamlet.

We learn all of this from the order of two little words. An eye and ear for these nuances is what one critic calls the "histrionic sensibility."

The term "histrionic sensibility" was coined by the American critic Francis Fergusson in his 1949 book *The Idea of a Theatre*. The histrionic sensibility is the ability to read a play for its three-dimensionality. It is the ability to read a script the way a musician reads a score, or an architect a blueprint—as an implication of a past or future three-dimensional event.

Fergusson writes: "The trained ear perceives and discriminates sounds; the histrionic sensibility (which may also be trained) perceives and discriminates *actions* [emphasis mine]."

Just as a musician interprets a complex score in order to play the music accurately and with feeling, we must interpret the text of a play accurately and in a way that moves an audience.

Theatre in general, and Shakespeare in particular, is not two-dimensional literature that walks but three-dimensional character in action. Developing the voice that allows us to see and hear the three-dimensionality of a play's structure is one of the most important skills necessary in the theatre.

To continue Fergusson's analogy with music and architecture for a moment, the difference between a symphony in the key of C major and one in C minor is "just" a few flats in the key signature. The difference between a window and a door is "just" a couple of centimeters on a blueprint. The difference between Hamlet and Iago is "am I" as opposed to "I am." If a musician struggles to play every note accurately and an architect labors to have each angle in alignment, why shouldn't we in the theatre labor over the meaning, sense, placement, and potential of every word we use? As Harley

Granville-Barker, the great British director, wrote, "the imagining of a play in action is, under no circumstances, an easy thing." Not easy, perhaps, but essential. "If we are to make Shakespeare our own again," he wrote, "we must all be put to a little trouble about it. . . . The tunes that he writes, the whole great art of his music making, we can master. Actors can train their ears and tongues and can train our ears to it. Our faculties rust with disuse and by misuse are coarsened, but they quickly recover delight in a beautiful thing."

You will need all the tools at your disposal to bring a play to three-dimensional life. My previous remarks notwithstanding, what follows should show you the value of research in informing your histrionic sensibility.

Here are the last four lines of *King Lear*:

The weight of this sad time we must obey,
Speak what we feel, not what we ought to say.
The oldest hath borne most. We that are young
Shall never see so much, nor live so long.

Who says them?

The 1608 Quarto text assigns the lines to the Duke of Albany, husband of one of Lear's daughters. The 1623 Folio (probably based on revised productions of the play, and published after Shakespeare's death) gives the speech to Edgar, the good son of the Duke of Gloucester. But whoever says the final lines, he has an important impact on the meaning of the play. How do you decide which "Shakespeare" is right? You can play only one a night!

There is no right or wrong answer here, but my vote goes to Edgar. He appears to be younger than Albany, who is not clever enough to lead this post-apocalyptic Celtic Britain. Moreover I think Albany knows this; he sees himself as a member of the older generation, not the younger. But a case could be made for either, depending on your interpretation of the evidence, including the type of men Lear's daughters would marry—their age, virility, wealth, etc.

What kind of "flesh" does Hamlet have (in I:2)? Is it "sallied," "sullied," or "solid"? Which word is actually Shakespeare's? The same with Ophelia's "sweet bells" (in III:1). Are they "jangled," out of "tune," or out of "time"? Is there a difference in meaning or is this merely an Elizabethan printer's error? How can we know what the words really mean if we can't be sure what the words really are?

In publishing a text or commentary, editors have their cake and eat it too. They have the liberty to discuss all the possibilities and levels of meaning and to list many variants in their footnotes. But in performance you must choose only one and play it. And the more information you bring to your decision-making, the richer your choices will be.

A filmmaker friend of mine who hated going to plays used to say that the theatre "was the last bastion of the amateur." I didn't admit it at the time, but I think he was partly right. We rely heavily on luck and emotion in the theatre, and often forget there is a job to do, a craft to master, and a story to tell.

There are dozens of "frog overlays" you can create yourself for work on the language—vowels, consonants, speed, imagery, musicality, end rhymes, and meter (which we will discuss in a moment). The work of making your work more textured and more layered never ends. The learning, the discovery never stops. So, at the very least, know what the words really mean!

· 3 ·

Whose Frog Is It
Anyway?

BEFORE WE CONTINUE the autopsy of our dead frogs, let me briefly address the Shakespeare "authorship" question.

There are two authorship debates going on within the Shakespeare world all the time. The first concerns the identity of the person who wrote the plays—whether Shakespeare, Marlowe, Bacon, or the Earl of Oxford. While this debate is largely irrelevant to the work we do, it sometimes raises interesting questions about the texts. How, for instance, did Shakespeare come to know so much about law, medicine, Italian, Latin, Greek, and geography?

Shakespeare lived in the most exciting city in Europe, in one of the most exciting political and economic eras ever. His theatre was on the Thames, near the docks and near the centers of power. News, fashion, rumors, and plots flowed outside his window. All he had to do was be a little curious. And if he found a story or theme he liked, say, in Plutarch's *Lives of the Romans* or Holinshed's *Chronicles of England*, he stole it and reworked it as his own! Like any good, working writer, Shakespeare probably was infinitely practical—he did his research. He hung out, talked to people, and above all, asked questions.

There is the story, probably apocryphal, that Shakespeare was forced to leave Stratford as a young man for poaching, that is, stealing, game. My theory of literary poaching at least makes him consistent. And it is far more sensible than believing that Marlowe faked his own death in a barroom brawl in order to grow up and become Shakespeare. I know this is heretical, especially in a book about Shakespeare. But the work we have to do in interpreting the texts and bringing them to life before a modern audience is the same even if the heavens opened and informed us that Sir Walter Raleigh wrote the plays. For our purposes, it really doesn't matter who wrote them.

The second authorship question touches on a politically sensitive area.

There is a great deal of discussion, particularly in academic and educational circles, about whether or not "Shakespeare the author" and "Shakespeare the texts" are racist, sexist, anti-Semitic, fascist, and homophobic. These arguments rage on and produce many opinions but few conclusions. One may, perhaps rightly, spend a lot of time on these issues, and they will certainly affect one's reading of a text. While I don't wish to minimize these arguments or the passions with which they are expressed, it is not the function of this book to respond to them.

My advice is simply not to limit yourself or your imagination, creativity, and artistic freedom, by limiting the possibilities of the text. There is no way, simply given the material at hand, that we can draw final conclusions about Shakespeare's meanings.

The French critic Roland Barthes once said that "He who

speaks is not he who writes, and he who writes is not he who is." In other words, Hamlet speaking is not Shakespeare, and Shakespeare writing is not Shakespeare, the man, having a beer.

As we study, explore, and encounter these plays, all of us must decide for ourselves whether Shakespeare's texts are timeless works of genius or outdated sexist tracts. Perhaps the truth lies somewhere in between, a complicated combination of good and bad. A very human combination, indeed.

Whatever we decide, we still face the challenge of asking ourselves why and how the plays should be done. Do the plays speak to us today? Or do we produce them simply because we can do so without paying royalties; or because they are "classics"?

These are the hard questions, the three-dimensional decisions that you, the artist, must make every day. They are your right, your privilege, and your responsibility. They are the essence of interpretation.

· 4 ·

Exercise Monologues

THE FOLLOWING MONOLOGUES are exercises, not audition pieces. Never perform a monologue or soliloquy unless you've studied the entire play from which it is drawn and understand fully its function in the play.

Take your time with these six speeches. Take them apart, slowly and carefully, doing your frog overlays and using the Shakespeare Paradigm.

I've placed them here so that you can work out the technical problems we've covered in the first three chapters. Don't perform them, just work on them. Take the engine apart and put it back together before you race the car. Later, as you approach performance, you'll return to them with greater skill and deeper meaning.

A Note for Actresses

Shakespeare's work is notorious for its scarcity of women's roles, especially minor ones. There is no need in this exercise to play the following characters as men unless you choose to. I encourage actors to explore female characters in like manner.

The Captain's "Bloody Sergeant" speech from *Macbeth*, Act I, scene 2.

> Doubtful it stood,
> As two spent swimmers that do cling together
> And choke their art. The merciless Macdonwald
> (Worthy to be a rebel, for to that
> The multiplying villainies of nature
> Do swarm upon him) from the western isles
> Of Kernes and Gallowglasses is supplied;
> And Fortune, on his damned quarrel smiling,
> Show'd like a rebel's whore. But all's too weak,
> For brave Macbeth (well he deserves that name),
> Disdaining Fortune, with his brandish'd steel,
> Which smok'd with bloody execution,
> Like Valour's minion, carv'd out his passage,
> Till he fac'd the slave;
> Which ne'er shook hands, nor bade farewell to him,
> Till he unseam'd him from the nave to th' chops,
> And fix'd his head upon our battlements.

Gertrude's "There is a willow" speech from *Hamlet*, Act IV, scene 7.

> There is a willow grows askant the brook
> That shows his hoary leaves in the glassy stream.
> Therewith fantastic garlands did she make
> Of crow-flowers, nettles, daisies, and long purples,
> That liberal shepherds give a grosser name,
> But our cold maids do dead men's fingers call them.
> There on the pendent boughs her crownet weeds
> Clamb'ring to hang, an envious sliver broke,
> When down her weedy trophies and herself
> Fell in the weeping brook. Her clothes spread wide,

And mermaid-like awhile they bore her up,
Which time she chanted snatches of old lauds,
As one incapable of her own distress,
Or like a creature native and indued
Unto that element. But long it could not be
Till that her garments, heavy with their drink,
Pull'd the poor wretch from her melodious lay
To muddy death.

Proteus's speech from *Two Gentlemen of Verona*, Act II, scene 6.

To leave my Julia, shall I be forsworn;
To love fair Silvia, shall I be forsworn;
To wrong my friend, I shall be much forsworn.
And ev'n that power which gave me first my oath
Provokes me to this threefold perjury.
Love bade me swear, and Love bids me forswear.
O sweet-suggesting Love, if thou hast sinn'd,
Teach me (thy tempted subject) to excuse it.
At first I did adore a twinkling star,
But now I worship a celestial sun:
Unheedful vows may heedfully be broken,
And he wants wit that wants resolvèd will
To learn his wit t'exchange the bad for better.
Fie, fie, unreverend tongue, to call her bad
Whose sovereignty so oft thou hast preferr'd,
With twenty thousand soul-confirming oaths.
I cannot leave to love; and yet I do;
But there I leave to love, where I should love.
Julia I lose, and Valentine I lose;
If I keep them, I needs must lose myself;
If I lose them, thus find I by their loss:
For Valentine, myself; for Julia, Silvia.

I to myself am dearer than a friend,
For love is still most precious in itself,
And Silvia (witness heaven that made her fair)
Shows Julia but a swarthy Ethiope.
I will forget that Julia is alive,
Rememb'ring that my love to her is dead.
And Valentine I'll hold an enemy,
Aiming at Silvia as a sweeter friend.
I cannot now prove constant to myself,
Without some treachery us'd to Valentine.
This night he meaneth with a corded ladder
To climb celestial Silvia's chamber-window,
Myself in counsel, his competitor.
Now presently I'll give her father notice
Of their disguising and pretended flight;
Who, all enrag'd, will banish Valentine,
For Thurio he intends shall wed his daughter.
But Valentine being gone, I'll quickly cross,
By some sly trick, blunt Thurio's dull proceeding.
Love, lend me wings to make my purpose swift
As thou hast lent me wit to plot this drift.

Rosalind's speech from *As You Like It*, Act III, scene 5.

And why, I pray you? Who might be your mother,
That you insult, exult, and all at once,
Over the wretched? What though you have no beauty—
As by my faith I see no more in you
Than without candle may go dark to bed—
Must you be therefore proud and pitiless?
Why, what means this? Why do you look on me?
I see no more in you than in the ordinary
Of Nature's sale-work. 'Od's my little life,
I think she means to tangle my eyes too!

No, faith, proud mistress, hope not after it.
'Tis not your inky brows, your black silk hair,
Your bugle eyeballs, nor your cheek of cream
That can entame my spirits to your worship.
You foolish shepherd, wherefore do you follow her
Like foggy South puffing with wind and rain?
You are a thousand times a properer man
Than she a woman. 'Tis such fools as you
That makes the world full of ill-favour'd children.
'Tis not her glass but you that flatters her,
And out of you she sees herself more proper
Than any of her lineaments can show her.
But mistress, know yourself. Down on your knees
And thank heaven, fasting, for a good man's love;
For I must tell you friendly in your ear,
Sell when you can, you are not for all markets.
Cry the man mercy, love him, take his offer;
Foul is most foul, being foul to be a scoffer.
So take her to thee, shepherd. Fare you well.

Coriolanus's speech from *Coriolanus*, Act IV, scene 5.

My name is Caius Martius, who hath done
To thee particularly, and to all the Volsces,
Great hurt and mischief: thereto witness may
My surname, Coriolanus. The painful service,
The extreme dangers, and the drops of blood
Shed for my thankless country, are requited
But with that surname: a good memory
And witness of the malice and displeasure
Which thou should'st bear me. Only that name remains.
The cruelty and envy of the people,
Permitted by our dastard nobles, who
Have all forsook me, hath devour'd the rest;

And suffer'd me by th' voice of slaves to be
Whoop'd out of Rome. Now this extremity
Hath brought me to thy hearth, not out of hope
(Mistake me not) to save my life: for if
I had fear'd death, of all the men i'th' world
I would have 'voided thee; but in mere spite
To be full quit of those my banishers,
Stand I before thee here. Then if thou hast
A heart of wreak in thee, that wilt revenge
Thine own particular wrongs, and stop those maims
Of shame seen through thy country, speed thee straight,
And make my misery serve thy turn: so use it
That my revengeful services may prove
As benefits to thee, for I will fight
Against my canker'd country with the spleen
Of all the under fiends. But if so be
Thou dar'st not this, and that to prove more fortunes
Th'art tir'd, then, in a word, I also am
Longer to live most weary, and present
My throat to thee and to thy ancient malice;
Which not to cut would show thee but a fool,
Since I have ever follow'd thee with hate,
Drawn tuns of blood out of thy country's breast,
And cannot live but to thy shame, unless
It be to do thee service.

Joan la Pucelle's speech from *Henry VI, Part 1*, Act I, scene 2.

Dauphin, I am by birth a shepherd's daughter,
My wit untrain'd in any kind of art.
Heaven and our Lady gracious hath it pleas'd
To shine on my contemptible estate.
Lo, whilst I waited on my tender lambs,

And to sun's parching heat display'd my cheeks,
God's Mother deigned to appear to me,
And in a vision full of majesty
Will'd me to leave my base vocation
And free my country from calamity.
Her aid she promis'd, and assur'd success.
In complete glory she reveal'd herself;
And, whereas I was black and swart before,
With those clear rays which she infus'd on me
That beauty am I blest with you may see.
Ask me what question thou canst possible,
And I will answer unpremeditated.
My courage try by combat, if thou dar'st,
And thou shalt find that I exceed my sex.
Resolve on this: thou shalt be fortunate
If thou receive me for thy warlike mate.

· 5 ·

Know Where the Play Is Going—Structure

FOR CENTURIES, critics and playwrights have struggled with Aristotle's definitions of drama and tragedy. In his formula, a play should present only certain themes and types of characters, and revolve around "unities" of structure. Even today, most Hollywood writers follow a precise Aristotelian formula for determining what action should occur on pages 1, 10, 30, 60, 90, and 120 of a screenplay.

But Shakespeare's plays were never "well-made" in this Aristotelian sense. His action is rough and tumble, illogical and emotional. Often, as in the histories, he compresses events that occurred over decades and makes them appear as if they happened overnight. *The Winter's Tale* has a sixteen-year gap in it. The Fool simply disappears in the middle of *King Lear.* There is no logical way Desdemona might have had an affair with Michael Cassio, since they were on Cyprus together for less than a day!

In their own time, Shakespeare's plays were criticized for being crude and vulgar. In the eighteenth and nineteenth centuries there were many rewrites of Shakespeare's plays in which the verse and plots were smoothed out and "civilized." My favorite example is the version of *King Lear* in which Lear and Cordelia live happily ever after. Shakespeare was regarded as a rugged and romantic genius who would have been so much better if he had only followed the rules!

If Shakespeare's plays are not "well-made," how were they put together? Critics have tried to discern various structures in them—propagandist, libertarian, proto-Marxist, absurdist, etc. But there is no evidence that Shakespeare, unlike Brecht or Racine, for example, wrote with a particular set of critical rules in mind. It appears he simply tried to tell a particular story in the best way he could, or in a better way than he found it in earlier sources.

Shakespeare wrote in an era of great cultural upheaval. The economic, political, religious, and social hierarchies that had bound the European world for more than fifteen hundred years ("the great chain of being" as E. M. W. Tillyard called it) were rapidly crumbling.

The resulting tension between personal fulfillment and social responsibility is at the core of Shakespeare's plays.

Whether it is Hermia running into the Athenian forest or Henry Bolingbroke pulling Richard II off the throne, the themes of individual ambition, risk, and reward propel many of the plays.

Macbeth risks everything from his marriage to his soul in order to become king. Hamlet risks his sanity to avenge his father. Juliet risks her life for Romeo, and so on. In the world of the comedies, the risk always pays off, as, for example, in Hermia's flight into the forest and her happy marriage in the end. In the history plays, the question of who has the personal and moral authority to rule—those who are born to the throne or those who are willing to risk taking it—drives the actions of the Richards, Henrys, and dukes of York, Gloucester, and Lancaster. In the problem plays and romances, such as *Measure for Measure* and *The Winter's Tale*, the risks are more complex, the rewards more subtle. Is a nun's chastity worth her brother's life? How much must a jealous husband suffer before he risks reconciliation?

In Elizabethan England, these were not idle questions. In Shakespeare's day a man or woman could journey to the New World and return rich, or lose his head for conspiring against the Crown. Is it any wonder that contracts—social and legal—abound in these plays?

I'm not suggesting that Shakespeare arose in the morning and said, "Aha! I'm living in early modern England, one of the great epochs of Western history. Let's see what I can write about it today." He was, above all, an infinitely practical playwright who relied as much on Renaissance theatrical practice as he did on contemporary politics and economics.

Instant Analysis, or Shakespeare Made Easy

The structures of Shakespeare's plays, for many complex cultural, political, and historical reasons, tend to conform to a single pattern. This "instant" structure occurs consistently in the plays and can be used as a road map for understanding most of them. Even in those plays where this structure doesn't quite apply, their deviation from the pattern provides helpful information. In short, here is an "instant" guide to Shakespeare's structure.

1. When the play begins, the world is in chaos.

2. There is an inadequate solution imposed by a duke or king, resulting in:

3. A rebellion against that duke or king (successful in comedy, unsuccessful in tragedy), leading to:

4. The installation of a new (or renewed) duke or king, but resulting in a less satisfying resolution for the world of the play.

This is the "order/disorder/rebellion—yes? no?—2nd order" of my 3 x 5 cards. Let me show you what I mean by analyzing several plays.

Macbeth:

Disorder: The opening revolt and the Thane of Cawdor's treason.

Order 1: Duncan's victory; Macbeth's reward of Cawdor's title; Scotland at (momentary) peace.

Rebellion: Macbeth's move for power and the throne; murders and civil war ensue.

Successful? No. Although he is king for a while, Macbeth is ultimately defeated and beheaded. Therefore the play is a tragedy.

Order 2: Malcolm, one of Duncan's sons, is enthroned as the rightful king of Scotland.

While there is a legitimate restoration of "order" within the world of the play, no one I know has ever been satisfied by it. We wish either that Macbeth had not gone wrong or that someone else, most likely Macduff, had taken charge. No one really wants Malcolm to become king, and no one is particularly satisfied by his coronation.

Romeo and Juliet:

Disorder: The opening brawl and the Montague/Capulet feud.

Order 1: The Duke of Verona orders an end to the fighting, or the Montagues and Capulets will pay with their lives. The Capulets throw a ball; Romeo and his friends attend so that he can see his true love, Rosaline. Everyone seems happy. Then:

Rebellion: Romeo and Juliet fall in love, defying everyone and everything.

Successful? No. Many people die, including the two lovers.

Order 2: Peace is restored by order of the Duke, who, renewed, now knows the truth of Romeo and Juliet's love. The families agree to build a gold monument to honor their children.

In terms of "satisfaction," do you think this is what the two teenagers would want? Obviously, they would rather have lived their lives together in peace. One of the distinctions between comedy and tragedy is that in a comedy everyone gets what they want, i.e., a happy ending; and in a tragedy everyone gets what they deserve—fate, if you will. This raises issues as to whether Romeo and Juliet *do* anything to deserve what happens to them, or whether they are complicit in their own demise.

A Midsummer Night's Dream:

This gets tricky, so hold on! First you must subdivide *A Midsummer Night's Dream* into three worlds: the real world of Theseus, Hippolyta, and the lovers; the fairy world of Oberon, Titania, and Puck; and the mechanical or rustic world of Bottom and Peter Quince.

The events in each of these worlds follow the formula I have outlined above. These parallel structures then combine to create an overarching formula for the entire play. The play's dynamic energy comes from the complex mixing and matching of events from among the three worlds.

Francis Fergusson, in *The Idea of a Theatre*, calls this kind of counterpoint "analogous action." He means that the play moves forward by comparison and contrast, as if it were a rotating prism or kaleidoscope. This process of changing points of view to reveal new facets (montage, in film) gives the audience new insight and perspective on each scene and its relationship to the whole.

In the development of a play's forward motion, as in *Macbeth* or *Hamlet*, invisible daggers and player kings are contrasted to genuine ones. The goddess Nature in Edmund's monologue is connected to the nature of the storm on the heath, the nature of love, the nature of human beings, and the natural order of all things throughout *King Lear*. Perhaps the most famous example of analogous action is the relationship of the avenging sons—Hamlet, Laertes, and Fortinbras—in *Hamlet*. The actions of each son shed light on the others, and on the larger themes in the play.

This process of comparing and contrasting is one of the great rhetorical engines driving Shakespeare's plays. Analogous action includes apposition and balance, antithesis and contrast. Almost everything in a Shakespearean play is compared to everything else: mercy to a pound of flesh; Rosaline to Juliet; Macbeth to Duncan; Malcolm to Macduff. Not until you reach the end of a text can you fully understand what the beginning and middle have been about. The building of relationships, their juxtaposition and arrangement, help us understand each individual moment, each event. That is why we need the road map of "instant" analysis and structure—to enable us to see the forest of the action through the trees of language.

In *A Midsummer Night's Dream* we contrast the reality of Athens to the fantasy world of the woods: Helen to Hermia; Lysander to Demetrius; Oberon to Theseus; and Titania to Hippolyta. We compare real love to that which is only dreamed of, and Pyramus and Thisbe to all lovers.

Here is an "instant analysis" of the three parallel worlds of *A Midsummer Night's Dream*:

Theseus's "Real" World: *Disorder:* Hermia refuses to marry the man her father has chosen for her. *Order 1:* Duke Theseus orders her to obey her father or face punishment. *Rebellion:* She runs off with her lover. *Successful?* Eventually. A comedy. *Order 2:* The happy Duke Theseus has them all marry and live happily ever after!

Oberon's "Fairy" World: *Disorder:* The fairy world is in an uproar as Oberon and Titania feud over rights to a boy. *Order 1:* Oberon puts a spell on Titania to get what he wants and to punish her. *Rebellion:* The potion used to make the spell falls into the wrong hands. *Successful?* Yes. All get what they want. Also a comedy. *Order 2:* Oberon, moved to pity, gives up his claim to the boy; he and Titania reconcile and bless the mortals' marriages.

Quince's "Mechanical" World: *Disorder:* Bottom tries to take over the rehearsals, jeopardizing their chances to play at the Duke's wedding feast. *Order 1:* Quince hands out parts and assigns roles as planned. *Rebellion:* Bottom, turned into an "ass," ruins the rehearsal. Believing he's dead, they call off their play. *Successful?* Yes, because it was only a dream and nobody dies. *Order 2:* Quince regroups, they mount the play, and it's a hit!

Now, the structure of the *entire* play goes like this:

Disorder: Hermia disobeys her father and flees into the woods, where the fairy king and queen are feuding and the "mechanicals" are trying to rehearse a play.

Order 1: Imposed by "king" Oberon. He orders Puck to put the love potion into Titania's eyes and into those of one of the mortals. Puck scares off the mechanicals by turning Bottom into an ass and leaving him to be discovered by Titania.

Rebellion: The wrong Athenians fall in love with one another, and Titania enjoys herself with an "ass"! Successful? Yes, because the spells are corrected and the right lovers wind up with one another. But it was close!

Order 2: Imposed by Duke Theseus. He commands everyone to be married and selects Quince's play for the wedding festivities. Then, all parties being amused and rewarded, they go off to bed so that the fairies may bless their nuptials with healthy children.

Note that even if you interpret the play more darkly—that rebellion is not successful because imposed marriage signifies an end to the lovers' youthful exuberance, innocence, and independence—the pattern of "instant analysis" still holds.

"Instant analysis" works because it seeks patterns already present within the plays instead of imposing a critical bias on them. We're not trying to fit Aristotle, Marx, Freud, Derrida, or Lacan into Shakespeare. At the moment it is enough that Shakespeare fit into Shakespeare! When we try in performance to squeeze one of his texts into a particular critical theory, we wind up staging the footnotes to the play, not the play itself!

Some critics would argue that my belief in an overriding

structure in Shakespeare's plays is a meaningless, intentionalist fallacy—that we cannot possibly discern Shakespeare's intentions as a playwright. The texts, they would argue, are so fluid and filled with slippages of meaning that all readings are relative, personal, and impermanent. This may be true for a private reading of a play done at a desk. In performance, however, a text becomes a fixed, communal event shared in public over time. If theatre has any social value, it consists in providing this shared experience to an audience. This is possible only if there is an apparent dramatic structure for all of us, on stage and off, to rely upon. I believe that through a rigorous analysis of Shakespeare's texts we can produce performances that are clear in their immediate outlines to an audience.

Most of us, fed on a diet of television, films, and the Internet, don't have the patience to see the beginning, middle, and end of a text and hold a part of it in our mind's eye and ear while we compare and contrast it to another part. If a text is daunting to you in pre-performance preparation, imagine how an audience feels when confronted by the entire text in one sitting.

In the practice of music and architecture, to employ Fergusson's analogies again, one must come to grips with objective, tangible realities relatively early in the creative process—notes on the page, dimensions on a drawing. Theatre, however, consists of fundamentally ephemeral events which evaporate even as they come into being. Theatre's challenge comes in trying to create a structure for these ephemera, so that they can live, breathe, and delight in performance. The goal is to provide a cathartic, moving, and emotional experience to the *audience*, not the actor. Keep that in mind as we resume work on the rhythm and sense of the line.

· 6 ·

Know the Rhythm and Sense of the Line— Character

SHAKESPEARE WROTE the bulk of his plays in iambic pentameter, a rhythm for speaking verse. It goes like this:

da-dum/da-dum/da-dum/da-dum/da-dum

An iamb is a "foot," or measure, of verse having a short/long shape: da-dum. There are other types of feet as well. A spondee is a foot with a long/long shape: dum-dum. A trochee has a long/short shape: dum-da. A dactyl has a long/short/short shape: dum-da-da. "Pentameter" means that the line contains five feet. There are other common line lengths in poetry. For example, the six-foot hexameter (the French classical line) was used by Racine and Corneille:

Noble et brilliant auteur d'une triste famille,
Toi, dont ma mére osait se vanter d'être fille,
Qui peut-être rougis du trouble ou tu me vois,
Soleil, je te viens voir pour la derniere fois.
                                          —Jean Racine, *Phaedre*

[63]

Most popular songs, including nursery rhymes and rhythm-and-blues, use a four-foot line (tetrameter).

Twinkle, twinkle little star
How I wonder what you are. . . .

If you're interested in more of this, a good place to start is with Samuel Taylor Coleridge's poem "Metrical Feet," which begins:

Trochee trips from long to short. From long
To long in solemn sort slow spondee stalks,
Strong foot, yet ill able ever to come up with
Dactyl tri-syllable. Iambics march from short to long.
With a leap and a bound the swift anapests throng. . . .

Most of Shakespeare's lines, however, are written in the short/long heartbeat of iambic pentameter:

Oh-what/a-rogue/and-peas/ant-slave/am-I

I call this Dumb Shakespeare (da-dumb, da-dumb, da-dumb). It can also be a very useful "frog overlay" for extracting the sense and meaning from a line.

Dumb Shakespeare

Practicing Dumb Shakespeare gives you an indication of the words and phrases the author wants stressed and the ones he wants played with a lighter touch. It also hints at how words are pronounced and the number of syllables sounded in certain words. This is not a hard and fast rule, but it is another "instant" technique for finding layers of meaning in a text. Here is the first part of Hamlet's speech again, in "Dumb" Shakespeare. Say these lines out loud:

Oh what/a rogue/and peas/ant slave/am I
Is it/not mon/strous that/this play/er here
But in/a fic/tion in/a dream/of passion [oops!]
Could force/his soul/so to/his own/conceit. . . .

What does saying the verse this way reveal? It tells us that
the "pez" in "peasant" is almost spat out with stress, even
though it's an adjective. It also emphasizes the comparison of
the nouns "slave" and "player" and forces us to confront an
irregular line:

But in/ a fic/tion, in/ a dream/ of pass-ion

The stress, if you read the meter as you would ordinarily,
is on the two "in's": "in" a fiction, "in" a dream of passion.
How many syllables are there in "pash-y-on"? It has to be
crammed (with passion!) into the last foot of the line, forcing
you to come up for air before going on to the next line
where, again, you encounter the question of the stress on
"to" in the third beat. You would probably, ultimately and
naturally, stress the nouns "fiction," "dream," and "passion," but Dumb Shakespeare allows you to consider alternative readings. And the consideration of alternatives is crucial
in developing both a pre-performance reading and a performance.

I like using Dumb Shakespeare early on because it con-
fronts the performer with the rhythms and intricacies of each
and every line. Nothing is more boring than listening to an
entire performance of sing-song iambic pentameter.

Dumb Shakespeare is a simple and practical tool that allows you to know immediately if there is a "hiccup" in a line.
It quickly tells you that attention must be paid and that regularity of meter cannot be assumed just because it's Shakespeare.

If you pay attention, Shakespeare's lines should swing like the best Dixieland jazz ("soul so to his own conceit" is a good example). The verse will bop and boogie all over the place!

On Rhythm

Do you remember what 4/4 or common time is? In it, there are four beats to the measure, and a quarter note gets one beat. Just recall "Here Comes the Bride" and "Pomp and Circumstance." As you march up the aisle, you step off on every other beat: 1-2-3-4; 1-2-3-4. This is not very musical, but it does show you where the beats are. Dumb Shakespeare does the same thing.

Now, jazz, blues, and rock are generally in 4/4 time, but the beat is hidden, syncopated, "jazzed up." Most of Shakespeare's verse shares this syncopation. Even the early plays, such as *Love's Labours Lost*, have a swing to them despite the almost formulaic regularity of the verse. Say these three well-known lines using Dumb Shakespeare first:

So foul/and fair/a day/I have/not seen

Friends Ro/mans coun/try men/lend me/your ears

The qual/ity/of mer/cy is/not strained

No one wants to perform the lines this way. (This is pre-performance work, remember.) But apart from helping you memorize the lines more quickly, look at what nuances of meaning this simple exercise evokes.

In the first, Macbeth sees the "foulness" in a day before he sees its "fairness," which might indicate something important about his character. In the second, the stress is on lending your ears to Marc Antony and not to Brutus. And, finally, in the third, the "quality" of mercy is stressed, as opposed to mercy itself. This forces a lawyerly pause after "is" and before "not strained," putting the entire courtroom in great suspense.

Read the lines aloud "dumb" a couple of times, sticking to the metronomic beat of the iambic pentameter, no matter how awkward. Then, just read them as if (oh, dear!) they were in modern, everyday English sentences. No acting, please. Just read the lines aloud:

So foul and fair a day I have not seen

Friends, Romans, countrymen, lend me your ears

The quality of mercy is not strained

That wasn't so hard, was it? The lines make sense. They're easier to say now and easier to listen to. And the syncopated mix of trochees and dactyls ("Romans, countrymen") comes more naturally to the voice. Instant Shakespeare! Voila!

Not So Dumb Shakespeare: Line Endings and Parallel Motion

There is a good deal of opinion on how to handle the last word in a line of iambic pentameter. Is it stressed? Run on to the next line? Is it a masculine (strong) ending or feminine (weak) one? (I didn't coin these terms!)

Shakespeare wrote primarily in iambic pentameter for two reasons. First, the five-foot line was the approximate length of a clause in spoken Elizabethan English. Even today, iambic pentameter pervades English:

I think/I am/too sick/to go/to school.
I want/to be/at home/and stay/in bed!

But for many reasons (television, computers, poor education), English sentences have, in general, become either short sound bites or rambling wrecks of bureaucratic and academic obfuscation.

The Last Word

What does this have to do with end words? The Elizabethans, who conducted most of their social discourse orally, were adept at listening. They were highly attentive to key words which would lead them in the direction the speaker was headed and connect the coming thought to the previous one. Remember, the Elizabethans came to "hear" a play, not see one.

In *Love's Labours Lost*, *A Midsummer Night's Dream*, and *Romeo and Juliet*, where the verse is formally constructed, end words form a springboard for moving the rhetorical argument forward; line endings are employed by the speakers to keep the listener's attention focused.

When they first meet, the dialogue between Romeo and Juliet forms a fourteen-line sonnet in which the line endings can be played like the volley and serve in a good tennis match:

ROMEO: If I profane with my unworthiest *hand*
    This holiest shrine, the gentle sin is *this*:
    My lips, two blushing pilgrims, ready *stand*
    To smooth that rough touch with a tender *kiss*.

JULIET: Good pilgrim, you do wrong your hand too *much*,
    Which mannerly devotion shows in *this*:
    For saints have hands that pilgrims' hands do *touch*
    And palm to palm is holy palmers' *kiss*.

ROMEO: Have not saints lips, and holy palmers, *too*?

JULIET: Ay, pilgrim, lips that they must use in *prayer*.

ROMEO: O then, dear saint, let lips do what hands *do*:
　　 They pray. Grant thou, lest faith turn to *despair*.

JULIET: Saints do not move, though grant for prayer's *sake*.

ROMEO: Then move not, while my prayer's effect I *take*.
　　 Thus from my lips, by thine, my sin is *purged*.

JULIET: Then have my lips the sin that they have *took*.

ROMEO: Sin from my lips? O trespass sweetly *urged*.
　　 Give me my sin again.

JULIET: You kiss by the *book*.

The end words themselves add up to a highly condensed
set of images, a sort of Elizabethan haiku. As an exercise,
read the end words of each line and see what sense or feeling
you get from them:

Hand this/Stand kiss
Much this/Touch kiss
Too prayer/Do despair
Sake take/ Purge took
Urged . . . Book

Even here, in this most poetic of all love scenes, you must
ask yourself why the characters choose to speak in verse at
this moment. Why do they choose to rhyme those particular
words? What do they want from each other, and how will
they use the language to communicate those wants and needs
effectively? What is the play about? Make sense, not sound!

Sense and Sensibility

The second reason why Shakespeare wrote primarily in iambic pentameter was for ease of memorization. Here is a description from North's sixteenth-century prose translation of Plutarch's *Lives of the Romans*. It describes the moment in which Marc Antony first encounters Cleopatra as she sails down the Nile on a golden barge:

> . . . the poop whereof was of gold, the sails
> purple, and the oars of silver, which kept
> stroke in rowing after the sound of the music of
> flutes, hautboys, citherns, viols, and such
> other instruments as they played upon the barge.
> And now for the person of herself: she was laid
> under a pavilion of cloth of gold of tissue, and
> attired like the goddess Venus. . . .

And here is how Shakespeare sets the text into verse:

> The barge she sat in, like a burnish'd throne,
> Burn'd on the water. The poop was beaten gold;
> Purple the sails, and so perfumed that
> The winds were lovesick with them. The oars were silver,
> Which to the tune of flutes kept strokes and made
> The water which they beat to follow faster
> As amorous of her strokes. For her own person,
> It beggar'd all description. She did lie
> In her pavilion, cloth of gold of tissue,
> O'er picturing that Venus where we see
> The fancy outwork Nature. . . .

Doesn't the verse have a momentum that the prose narrative lacks? Go ahead. Read both selections to see which one works better for you. Remember to make the nouns sound like what they are. Put a slight stress on the last word in each line as if it were a springboard to the next. Don't be deceived by the punctuation—pause only when you need to breathe.

Sonnets and Monologues

All blank verse is not created equal. Sonnets are not monologues, and monologues are not poems. In general, I have excluded Shakespeare's sonnets from this study because they succeed primarily on literary, not dramatic, grounds. A sonnet is based upon a conceit, a central idea or metaphor. A dramatic monologue, in contrast, is based upon an argument that is connected to the greater themes of the play.

I have included a sonnet here in order to demonstrate the difference between the two forms. (In some of my workshops, I also use them as a way of introducing the possibilities of interpretation and personalization.)

The sonnet is a world unto itself, complete and self-referential. Certainly a sonnet can be made to appear dramatic—you can create a situation and a relationship in which to contextualize the poem—but its world is still personal and self-contained. The difference, then, lies in the application of the Shakespeare Paradigm. In a sonnet, the answer to the question "why, etc.?" is not to be found in the text but in the emotional and personal experience of the individual speaker.

I do not intend to slight the sonnets (or any of Shakespeare's other dramatic and narrative poems, such as *Venus and Adonis* or *The Rape of Lucrece*), but this book's emphasis is on acting and directing Shakespeare's plays, and we will return to them soon enough.

For now, though, go through the following sonnet, applying your "frog overlays" to its fourteen lines. Apply the

Shakespeare Paradigm. What is the emotional state of the speaker? Hint: the sonnet is one long sentence. If the speaker is sad at the beginning of the poem, is he still sad at the end? And if you don't know what "haply" really means, go running to your Onions!

Sonnet XXIX

When in disgrace with Fortune and men's eyes,
I all alone beweep my outcast state,
And trouble deaf heaven with my bootless cries,
And look upon myself and curse my fate,
Wishing me like to one more rich in hope,
Featured like him, like him with friends possessed,
Desiring this man's art, and that man's scope,
With what I most enjoy contented least;
Yet in these thoughts myself almost despising
Haply I think on thee, and then my state,
Like to the lark at break of day arising
From sullen earth, sings hymns at heaven's gate;
For thy sweet love remember'd such wealth brings,
That then I scorn to change my state with kings.

The Theatrical Event

The reconstruction of the Globe Theatre in London demonstrates two important elements of the conditions in which Shakespeare worked—the size of the audience and the size of the stage. Research conducted during its reconstruction revealed that the original Globe held between two and three thousand people. (Because of the addition of modern creature comforts and safety features, the new Globe holds only about half as many.) The stage is forty-four feet wide and twenty-five feet deep, with a twenty-eight-foot opening between the two pillars supporting the stage roof.

And unlike earlier versions of reconstructed Shakespearean theatres in which the stage thrusts into the audience, the London Globe stage sits like a rock-concert stage at the end of an arena. The stage length and position give the spectator a much more panoramic view of the action. To get some sense of the difference, imagine Mick Jagger running left to right across the front of the stage instead of up and down from front to back.

This configuration puts Shakespeare's stage solidly in the tradition of medieval pageant plays. What does this excursion into theatre history have to do with "playing the line"? The answer is this: given the architectural conditions of Shakespeare's theatre, it is impossible to perform his plays as Victorian grand operas or Freudian inner monologues. The plays must be performed as *events*.

An event occurs every time there is a change in a relationship on stage. Relationships exist in the theatre between one actor and another, between an actor and the audience, and within an actor and him/herself. Events are the turning points, the moments of impact in those relationships. These are the moments when decisions are made and risks taken. The structuring of events is the process by which we manifest human relationships on stage. This structuring is the essential, fundamental responsibility of the actor and director.

Many people believe that the narrative structure in Shakespeare is expressed through the verse. I believe that the impulse that *precedes* language is the true language of performance and the true language of Shakespeare. Let me see if I can give you an "instant" idea of what I mean.

Remember those silent-movie stars, Lillian Gish and

Mary Pickford, with their wide-eyed reactions to events? Impulses flashed across their faces before the dialogue cards appeared on the screen. If you had to choose, which would you rather see? A silent film of people and their reactions or a silent film of dialogue cards? You can take away language, but you can't take away impulse. Impulse precedes language; it is the heartbeat of a performance.

With that in mind, then: language is the least important element in Shakespeare! Before you start screaming, "How can he say that!," hear me out.

The first audiences for Shakespeare's plays were "Shakespeare virgins." They hadn't studied the plays in school, hadn't written term papers or been quizzed to death on them. Still they "got" the plays. How did they do it? Did everyone in Elizabethan England speak like Hamlet? What about those six or seven hundred words Shakespeare invented and added to the language? How did the audience follow Shakespeare's plays in the raucous atmosphere of the Elizabethan theatre? The answer is that they followed the *action*, not the words.

Language was used ultimately to tell a story, to portray the sweep of a large dramatic structure. Performances of Shakespeare's plays were not poetry readings. Both actor and audience became engaged in an event that was simple, direct, and immediate, in the same way a sporting event or rock concert might be today.

Shakespeare's audience did not know in advance that Lady Macbeth would go mad, that Hamlet would return to Elsinore, or that Shylock would insist on his pound of flesh. Wanting to find out what happened next, they paid close attention to the action, not the words. Actors communicated clearly and physically, and the story was instantly understood in the theatre. Elizabethan acting was a blood sport, like bear-baiting or cock-fighting, and Shakespeare's actors had enormous energy and presence.

When several of Britain's finest actors played scenes and sonnets from Shakespeare on the Globe stage during the 1995 prelude season, they rendered Shakespeare's language so overwrought with meaning and poetry that it sank, lifeless, into the groundlings' pit. Their inner monologues, filled with subtext, never made it past the edge of the stage. Frustrated that their old tricks and training didn't work, these actors wound up shouting a great deal. ("Can you hear me in the back, dear boy? It is the Bard, you know!") They played the new Globe as if it were a theatre with a roof and computerized lighting and sound, not realizing that their acting style was completely unsuited to the architecture.

Playing the action drives the Shakespearean line, whether verse or prose, and endows it with shape, strength, and muscularity. By playing the argument and the action we keep the line, and therefore the play, moving forward. We keep the event simple, direct, and immediate.

Sir Peter Hall, the great British director, once said that Shakespeare's language would be unintelligible to us in fifty years. I think he's wrong.

Shakespeare's language will disappear only if his stories—great stories of love, ambition, self-doubt, murder, revenge, betrayal, and foolishness—lose their meaning.

What we've lost today is the awareness that Shakespeare's plays are *events* created by means of language. Today we often read his plays not for their action but for their commentary. We impose culturally constructed readings onto them (feminist, postcolonial, new historicist) and wind up staging the footnotes to the plays and not the plays themselves!

Chapter Exercise

Here is Edmund's soliloquy from the first act of *King Lear*. In an audience of two thousand Anglo-Saxon males on a foggy afternoon in Elizabethan London, how many "bastards" were there? By the end of the speech, how many men were on their feet, cheering Edmund on?

Work through the speech with your frog overlays and pose the Shakespeare Paradigm: Why does this particular character say these particular words, in this particular order, at this particular moment?

> Thou, Nature, art my goddess; to thy law
> My services are bound. Wherefore should I
> Stand in the plague of custom and permit
> The curiosity of nations to deprive me
> For that I am some twelve or fourteen moonshines
> Lag of a brother? Why 'bastard'? Wherefore 'base'?
> When my dimensions are as well compact,
> My mind as generous, and my shape as true
> As honest madame's issue? Why brand they us
> With 'base', with 'baseness', 'bastardy'—base, base—
> Who, in the lusty stealth of nature, take
> More composition and fierce quality
> Than doth within a dull, stale tired bed
> Go to th' creating a whole tribe of fops,
> Got 'tween sleep and awake? Well, then,
> Legitimate Edgar, I must have your land.
> Our father's love is to the bastard Edmund
> As to th' legitimate. Fine word, 'legitimate'.
> Well, my legitimate, if this letter speed
> And my invention thrive, Edmund the base
> Shall top th' legitimate. I grow. I prosper.
> Now gods, stand up for bastards!

Do you see how the events—the changing relationships between Edmund, Nature, and the audience—are created? Edmund's language is simple, direct, and immediate, but also powerful, swift, and passionate. He is full of pent-up fire, anger, and desire. Your job is to communicate that to an audience by breathing only when you need to and letting the ideas carry you along with the longest possible line. Shakespeare's characters love their language. They choose marvelous, exciting words—not just "steeds" and "daggers" but "moonshine," "invention," and "top."

How many times have you actually seen Shakespeare's language communicated with passion and clarity on stage? In my experience it doesn't happen very often. In order to bring his characters and stories to life on stage, we must approach the texts as if we have never seen them before, as if we don't know how Shakespeare's stories end. The audience must hope Romeo arrives at Juliet's tomb before it is too late. They must want Lear and Cordelia to reconcile. They must find Shakespeare's jokes funny without being hit over the head with sight-gags and slapstick!

With your new understanding of the rhythm and shape of the lines, go back now and rework the "Exercise Monologues" in Chapter 4. Then proceed to Chapter 7 to begin work on pre-performance readings.

· 7 ·

Know What the Play Is About— Central Event

ONE OF THE MOST essential tasks when working on a play is determining, or better yet discovering, what the play is "about."

"About" does not mean the plot or theme but rather the central event that underlies the play's existence. It is the action that answers the question, "Why did this author write this play?" What lesson does the author want us to learn? What is he or she trying to tell us?

Tennessee Williams calls this the "outcry" of personal lyricism. What does Hamlet's "Oh, vengeance!" or Lear's "Howl, howl, howl, howl!" or Isabella's "Justice, justice, justice, justice!" signify? These are their outcries to us. For me, what the play is about is always conditioned by time and space; interpretation is about vision—how you see the play and its world, and how you see your own world.

I believe there is a correct way in which to analyze a play so that its meaning, its structure, becomes apparent. You cannot interpret the Ninth Symphony of Beethoven until you have analyzed and understood its harmonic structure. You cannot build your dream house unless you lay its foundation correctly. In the theatre, analysis is not a matter of opinion but of rigorous, sometimes tedious, word-by-word, line-by-line, scene-by-scene wrestling with the text. These tasks must be undertaken long before the performance begins.

Interpretation, however, is much more personal and problematic. There are no right or wrong interpretations, only ones that work or don't work. Interpretation is what differentiates Olivier's *Hamlet* from Kenneth Branagh's, Mel Gibson's, or Ethan Hawke's. The language and the structure are the same in each case, but the results, the interpretations, are unique.

Your interpretation depends upon your experience, knowledge, career, love life, who you are and where you are—all of it! These many factors will affect your encounter with the text and how you bring it to life before an audience. What I think about *Hamlet* today—the way I stage it and write about it—is entirely different from what I thought about the play ten years ago, or will think ten years from now. My vision reflects not only the elements within Shakespeare's text but also the human elements constantly changing around me. It is this complex combination of the evidence in the text and my own life experience that shapes my interpretation.

Interpretation implies a commitment to provisionality. All we can ask of the play and of ourselves is that we demonstrate what the play means to us at this particular moment in our lives. This means being present in the play in a very deep, committed, and vulnerable way. How can I, then, in this short chapter, presume to tell you what *Hamlet* or any of Shakespeare's plays is "about"? I can't. I can only offer you an "instant" guide to interpretation.

A Handy Note to Carry Around

A valid interpretation of a play develops from a premise, which in turn is derived from study and analysis. That premise is then challenged in rehearsal and tested in performance. If this sounds like the "scientific method," you're right. The theatre is a laboratory in which we test our ideas and ideals.

What follows, then, is a handy outline of that method—a Handy Note to Carry Around. Keep it in your pocket when you begin teaching or rehearsing the play. Refer to it during the day-in and day-out challenges of rehearsal to remind yourself of what you wanted to say, and why.

1. What is the end of the play?
2. What is the tune?
3. What is the texture?
4. What is the play about?

Could it be any more "instant"? Let's start with the easy one: What's the end?

The End—Dead Sea Scrolls

The end of the play is whatever is on the last page!

As obvious as this sounds, it is often forgotten or ignored—many productions of *Hamlet* end before Fortinbras arrives or cut him out completely. The end of a play is like a crime scene. What can we learn from the evidence at hand about why things ended up the way they did? Unlike in life, in a play we actually know in advance how the characters end up. Our job is to discover why. A way to look for clues is to play a game I call "Dead Sea Scrolls."

The Dead Sea Scrolls are parchment fragments of liturgical and scriptural texts written in Hebrew and Aramaic in the third century B.C. They were discovered in 1947 in caves near the ancient city of Qumran on the Dead Sea, a large salt lake in the Middle East. Since they are only fragments, they are subject to many varying interpretations by scholars of differing religious and political beliefs.

Suppose that instead of having the "Compleat Works" of William Shakespeare we had only a few "Dead Sea Scroll" fragments of the plays. What could we deduce or reconstruct about the plays, their author, and the world in which he lived? How might a study of these fragments influence our interpretations?

Take a look at the last page of *Hamlet*. Fortinbras tells four war-weary captains to

Bear Hamlet like a soldier to the stage,
For he was likely, had he been put on,
To have proved most royally; and, for his passage,
The soldiers' music and the rites of war
Speak loudly for him.
Take up the body: such a sight as this
Becomes the field, but here shows much amiss.
Go, bid the soldiers shoot.

A dead march. Exeunt, bearing off the bodies, after which a peal of ordnance is shot off.

What literary detective work can we do? We want to know who Fortinbras is and how he got there. We want to know how Hamlet died. Did Fortinbras slay him in battle? If not, who did and how? Why? Who are the other victims? Where does the action take place? What went so "amiss"? And whom is Fortinbras addressing?

Remember, we have only this fragment, the title of the play, and no truckfuls of library books. What can we deduce from this "Dead Sea Scroll"? We know that Fortinbras is in command because the soldiers do, indeed, shoot. There's something intriguing about setting *Hamlet* on the stage, but remember you know nothing at this point of the Players and the mousetrap. Look carefully at the line, "For he was likely, had he been put on/ To have proved most royally." What does this mean?

"Put on" I take to mean not only elevated to the throne but also tested (as in "put upon") by the challenges and responsibilities of kingship and leadership. Moreover "he would have proved most royally." Is Fortinbras merely saying the right things at a politic moment, or does he know his enemy? Would Hamlet have matured into greatness on the throne? There are intimations of large issues at work in this small fragment. These are the themes I would explore as I worked back through the play.

Hamlet (I'm cheating for a moment) doesn't escape a shipwreck at sea, send his two chums to be executed, and all the rest only to return to Elsinore to inevitable death in a swordfight. When an Elizabethan audience came to the theatre, they were not coming to see masterpieces and classics; they came to "hear a play" whose outcome they did not know. Even though Shakespeare retold stories that were well known to his audiences, they would be highly interested in how he did it. In some of the sources available to Shakespeare, for instance, the Hamlet character lives in the end. Wouldn't it be interesting to see a version of *Hamlet* in which his death actually came as a surprise in the final minutes of the play?

As another example, let's look at *A Midsummer Night's Dream*.

On the last page, the fairies, in an impressive torchlight entrance, enter the human world of Theseus to make sure that the wedding-night lovemaking of the three couples brings forth perfect babies. They steal away and then Puck enters and begs forgiveness for having (possibly) offended someone.

> If we shadows have offended,
> Think but this, and all is mended,
> That you have but slumber'd here
> While these visions did appear.
> And this weak and idle theme,
> No more yielding but a dream,
> Gentles, do not reprehend.
> If you pardon, we will mend.
> And, as I am an honest Puck,
> If we have unearned luck
> Now to 'scape the serpent's tongue,
> We will make amends ere long;
> Else the Puck a liar call.
> So, goodnight unto you all.
> Give me your hands, if we be friends,
> And Robin shall restore amends.

Why offended when we've been talking about sex all night long! Whom is he addressing? We want to know about the relationship of the fairies to the humans, what the "offence" might have been, and work from there to reconstruct the events which lead us to the "scene of the crime." What trails should you follow? I think you've got the idea by now. Let's go on to the next question, What's the tune?

Name That Tune

When I'm teaching my Instant Shakespeare workshops, this is my favorite part of the course, because I get to sing(?) in public, and no one can stop me!

Suppose you attend a performance of *Hello, Dolly!* The producers want the audience to leave the theatre humming the theme of the show, its "tune." They play it over and over again—as an overture, at intermission, in the key scenes, and at the curtain call. (I'm singing "Hello, Dolly" here.) If the audience leaves the theatre humming *another* tune from the show, say "Put on Your Sunday Clothes" (singing again), something's wrong. They're happy and they've enjoyed themselves, but they're humming the wrong tune! The production has put the emphasis in the wrong place.

Hello, Dolly! is about the impact of Dolly Levi's extraordinary life on everyone she meets. The "tune" of the show has to be about meeting her, about saying "hello" to Dolly.

Interestingly, when I ask my students what went wrong, they invariably say that "they" (meaning the audience) didn't get it. But what didn't the audience get? Who had six or eight weeks of rehearsal, the audience or the production? Who is seeing the material for the first time, the audience or the performers? Who is responsible for knowing and communicating the play's "tune"? It is the director, performers, designers, and producers.

What is the "tune" of *Macbeth*? What is the line, the word, the image that is repeated over and over again? "It will have blood, they say. Blood will have blood."

In *Macbeth* we have murders, executions, a bloody sergeant, bloody daggers, and witches and ghosts dipping and dripping in blood. Macbeth is steeped in "bloody instructions" and "bloody business." Lady Macbeth tries to wash away her "damned spot." At the end of the play Macbeth's head winds up on a bloody pole, and he and his Lady are called the "dead butcher and his fiend-like queen." It should come as no surprise that the tune is about blood. Remember that Kurosawa's film version of *Macbeth* is called *Throne of Blood*?

In most plays, however, the tune is not so obvious. What is the "tune" of *Hamlet*? What lines, words, and images keep recurring? The answer, curiously, has nothing to do with being or not being. Other than Hamlet, very few people in Elsinore give much thought to existential issues. (Claudius, surprisingly, is one of the few who do.)

There is something else that runs through the play, something everyone talks about. It is the most famous line in the play not spoken by Hamlet: "Something is rotten in the state of Denmark."

When the play begins, the rotting Ghost wanders the earth; old Norway rots, impotent in his bed; solid, sallied, or sullied flesh melts; things are "rank and gross" in nature; "cankers" gall the "infants of the spring"; old stock cannot be inoculated against disease and corruption; enseamed beds are "stewed in corruption"; and kisses are "reechy."

Hamlet's own rot, his inability to act, is at the core of the play. Returning to the final fragment of the text, would Hamlet have "proved most royally," or is he already too corrupted by his melancholia and impotence? He describes this condition as a "mole of nature," a cancer that destroys otherwise noble men.

In *Hamlet*, Shakespeare draws upon the Elizabethan analogy in which the king is to the state as the head is to the body (an example of analogous action). The "rot" within the two kings—old Hamlet's body corroded by poison and Claudius's more ambiguous moral rot—is directly responsible for the political, social, and moral decay of the country. There is "rank corruption" in Gertrude's hasty marriage to Claudius. The body of Polonius is left to rot under the staircase. And by Act V, all of Denmark is a marshy, boggy graveyard. Hamlet and Horatio slog through the muck toward an Elsinore where corpses and skulls now lurk just below the surface of the earth.

In the course of the play, Hamlet descends from the rarefied air of the battlements where he first meets the Ghost, to the open pit of Ophelia's grave. In the process, he gains an acceptance of death and with it an acceptance of what it means to be human.

Discover the tune of *A Midsummer Night's Dream* or *Romeo and Juliet* for yourself. (Hint: it might have something to with love at first sight, or stars and fire!) Then explore the problem of style, or rather, texture.

Texture

Alan Schneider, one of the theatre's great teachers and directors, used to say (only half jokingly) that style was "the distance between two actors."

He meant that when you stage a Greek tragedy, for example, the actors are at opposite ends of the stage. Then, as you proceed chronologically through Restoration comedy, Chekhov, Pinter, and David Mamet, the actors get closer and closer to one another as the plays become more realistic. Shakespeare, of course, is somewhere in the middle.

It was Alan who taught me to use the word "texture" rather than "style," because "texture" is tangible and three-dimensional. Texture is something you can hold in your hand, bring to a design meeting, and demonstrate to an actor in rehearsal. Texture is practical and real. Texture is the practical application of style.

What kind of blood do you want dripping in Macbeth's Scotland? What kind of "rot" infects Hamlet's Denmark? How do you show it? What's the texture of the moonlight in *Midsummer Night's Dream*? The texture of the forest? What kind of juice do you put in the lovers' eyes? What's the texture of young love that burns like a shooting star in *Romeo and Juliet*, and yet is surrounded by oppressive darkness and gloom? How do you show it?

When Fortinbras commands four soldiers to carry Hamlet off, what do those soldiers look like? How bloodied are they? How well armed? How "Norwegian"? What's the "texture" of the Witches in *Macbeth*? What kind of dagger does Macbeth pull out to match the invisible one? The list is endless—these are just a few of the many choices you must make to turn a dead text into a living one.

Let me put the problem another way: what's the texture of Hamlet's madness, Macbeth's ambition, or Titania's infatuation? Since you can't hold infatuation, ambition, and madness in your hand, you must find specific and tangible expressions of these concepts in color, fabric, and flesh and blood. Otherwise you run the danger of producing generic "Shakespearean" madness, ambition, or infatuation. What then is to be done? The solution lies in manifestation.

ON MANIFESTATION

Theatre is about the manifestation of human relationships.

There are two types of manifestation, or showing. The first is the purely physical manifestation of props, costumes, sets, and lights. Will Macbeth wear kilts, fur, or a Civil War uniform? Why? As we prepare for performance, even before we rehearse, we're trying to get a three-dimensional idea of a play that we can live with, day in and day out. Think of texture as the key signature in your music, or the color of your walls. Try out several keys and color chips to find the one that fits, the one that's right for you. Each decision brings you one step closer to your own interpretation of the play.

For example, to manifest my idea of "rot," I might decide to have the costumes in *Hamlet* look as if they've been gnawed by rats. Perhaps I'll have the set become increasingly "mucky" as each act progresses. Maybe I want thick, gooey blood in *Macbeth*, with bearlike men and dank, moss-covered walls. And maybe I'd want a warm night on a Greek island for my midsummer's "dream," with the fragrance of jasmine in the air to loosen my inhibitions.

Or not! We'll forget for a moment that the "muck" in *Hamlet* is totally impractical because the cleaning bill for the costumes would bankrupt the theatre! At least your mind is moving in the right direction, and that's what counts! Remember, there is no right and wrong, only what is valid or invalid for the entire play. Before making a final decision, I would test my rat-eaten "rot," or gooey blood, or Mediterranean island dream against the text, line by line and word for word. I would ask myself not only if it "works" but also if it is the *best* way to show the events and relationships that make up the play. Anything can be made to "work," so challenge yourself and your bright ideas; test your hypotheses.

The second, more important, type of manifestation concerns acting. Let me give you my definition of acting now, even though we will not put it into practice until we reach Part Two:

Acting is the organized and repeatable physical manifestation of an emotional state of being. The corollary to which is: acting is a study of the breath.

Acting is organized; you gather and process information, emotions, and activities and form them into a pattern to create a character. Acting is repeatable; you repeat these patterns in rehearsal, as they develop, and then in performance over the course of a run. An inner emotional state must exist for every moment you play. The task is to move the story forward by physically manifesting that inner life by means of external activities and actions.

How do Hamlet, Macbeth, and Titania show their madness, ambition, or infatuation in specific actions and details of behavior? How do they walk, pick up a fork, drive a car? How do they turn the pages of a newspaper over coffee in the morning? Which newspaper do they read? What kind of animal are they? Where is their center, their core? How do they hold themselves in public? Does it change when they are alone? And so on. The list of questions is nearly inexhaustible. The answers are found through "this, not that."

"THIS, NOT THAT"

Suppose that I am directing a production of *Macbeth*. I have already begun the "this, not that" process by deciding to produce *Macbeth* and not *Hamlet*. I continue this process by choosing designers A, B, and C rather than designers X, Y, and Z. I make a major "this, not that" decision by casting one actor out of hundreds to play Macbeth. Every decision I make is part of the process of "this, not that." The same is true for the actor playing Macbeth: suppose he decides that the Witches are in his head and do not exist in reality; that the dagger he sees is actually there; and that in "Tomorrow and tomorrow and tomorrow" there are long pauses after each "tomorrow." Each of these decisions is part of the process of "this, not that."

Finally, "this, not that" continues into the actual performance before an audience. In playing the text and the role, the actor must always give the character the freedom to "opt out," to choose *not* to do what is written. The possibility of an alternative action must always exist. The dagger speech must hold out the hope that Macbeth will walk away from the murder of Duncan before it is too late. The actor must always give his character the option of doing "this, not that."

In this way the events and emotions of the play are as unknown to us as they would be in life. In this way the outcome of the play becomes inevitable without being obvious. "This, not that" is, in effect, a provisional commitment to meaning, a temporary answer.

APPLYING "THIS, NOT THAT"

"This, not that" is a process of elimination, of ruling out choices and options, of choosing and selecting "rogue" not "bum"; "peasant slave" not "dirty slave"; "dagger" not "penknife"; and "steeds" not "nags." This choice-making process is at the heart of analysis and interpretation in performance. One builds a personal voice by the accretion and accumulation of selections, of "this, not that," by engaging in a process of discrimination.

For many good reasons, discrimination is a concept that has gone out of favor. But in this case discrimination is exactly what is required—selecting and eliminating, using one's taste, instinct, personal preference, research, study, and experience. This kind of discrimination implies that you, as the reader and performer, are prepared to take responsibility for your own interpretation of the play.

What Is the Play About?

Answering the question "What is the play about?" means looking for the "why" of the play. Why must Hamlet avenge his father's murder? Why must he treat Ophelia or his mother the way he does? Why is it better to suffer the slings and arrows of outrageous fortune? The answer can be elusive, frustrating, and different each time you look for it. At best, the answer will be merely provisional—the best you can do at that moment. But it results from your struggle with the text and your effort to build a logical, impassioned, and persuasive case for your reading, one step at a time. When I begin asking myself what the play is "about," I usually ask myself, "What's hidden in the sand?"

HIDDEN IN THE SAND

On my first visit to Kyoto, Japan, a friend and I visited various temples and monasteries. At one, we stopped to watch a Zen monk working at his morning sand sculpture. The monk walked around and around his box of sand, occasionally drawing his rake across it, until, ever so slowly, a shape began to emerge—an elegant leaf, with veins and a stem.

When the sculpture was complete, the monk allowed himself a sense of satisfaction in what he had helped to reveal in the sand that day. Somewhere in that three-dimensional box of sand the leaf had already existed, and the monk had helped to elicit it. He walked around the box, chatted about the leaf with visitors, and took one or two suggestions for changing it. Then, slowly and lovingly, he walked away from the leaf, knowing that the evening rains would certainly wash it away.

While I think this is a good metaphor for the impermanence of art and the artist's relationship to his or her creation, the most important thing is this: that particular leaf was what the sand was "about" that morning. It was the one and only thing that could be made manifest at that moment in that space by that particular artist.

This is an important analogy for our work in the theatre.

After weeks of pre-performance study and rehearsal, the play's meaning begins to emerge from the "sand" of the play's language. This is an exciting time in the rehearsal process, as our hard work in the process of "this, not that" begins to pay off and our ideas become increasingly clear.

In response to postmodernist critics who would argue that meanings of texts cannot be fixed, I would say that meaning in performance always becomes fixed, if only for the moment, if only provisionally. Like the monk's leaf, performance is ephemeral and has only a brief existence; and like the sand, "what the play is about" will change with our next encounter with the text. But every time I speak a line of text, it becomes fixed and concrete, even if only for that moment. I may release it, change it, and make it fluid again, but for that particular moment it is done with and must mean something; otherwise I am speaking nonsense. Similarly, the choices of designer, cast, and the shape of the stage each "fixes" the text in a particular way, bringing to it a specific, if provisional, meaning.

In Instant Shakespeare, when I ask myself what the play is about, I am looking for what's hidden in the sand of Shakespeare's language. Remember that earlier I said that language was the least important element in Shakespeare? Here, we are looking under the language for the impulse that creates the event, the impulse that answers the question, "why, etc.?"

Usually there is a hint in the title. Take *The Tragedy of Hamlet, Prince of Denmark*, for example. Hamlet, Prince of Denmark, fails to become Hamlet, King of Denmark. Why? Because, unlike Fortinbras or even Laertes, he refuses to play the roles life has assigned him—avenging son and gallant prince. In its search for meaning, every production of *Hamlet* must ultimately deal with why he acts, or, rather, doesn't act.

What Hamlet *Is About: An Instant Answer*

A prince was nothing if not Machiavellian in Shakespeare's day, and Hamlet, at the beginning of the play, is incapable of being Machiavellian. He cannot pretend, he cannot "seem": "Seems, Madame? Nay . . . I know not 'seems.'" He tells everyone in Elsinore how to act ("get thee to a nunnery," "speak the speech, I pray you"), but he himself cannot act. By the fifth act, however, Hamlet has learned his lesson—he is ready to out-act Laertes at Ophelia's grave, to drink vinegar, and eat a crocodile. "Nay . . . I'll rant as well as thou," he says. He has now accepted the role of Providence in the fall of the sparrow. What happened?

"Tis I, Hamlet, the Dane!" is Hamlet's declaration that he has returned, prepared to play the role in which life has cast him. *Hamlet* is a great debate on being and not being, but all debate comes to a halt when Hamlet finally accepts his part and his mortality. In every line of the play we must know why Hamlet first refuses to accept his role. Then, in the play's central event, we must know why he chooses that particular moment in which to accept his fate.

1. What is the end? Norway orders Hamlet's body carried off.
2. What is the tune? Something's rotten in Denmark.
3. What is the texture? Mucky rot.
4. What is the play about? Acceptance; "let be."

Played this way, *Hamlet*, the story of a young man who must face up to his destiny, becomes simple, direct, and immediate in spite of its classical status and the density (and even familiarity) of its language. In the Aristotelian sense, it might even be thrilling—inspiring the fear, pity, and terror that jolt us into awareness and understanding.

Chapter Exercise

Before you go on to Part Two, sit down with a Shakespeare play, preferably one that's unfamiliar to you, and read it through. Use the exercises from Part One to help you. See if, by the time you finish, you really know what the words mean; if you know the rhythm and sense of the lines; if you know where the play is going. Most of all, see if you can discover what the play is about by testing its end, tune, and texture through the process of "this, not that."

And Now?

And now we've come to the end of Part One. We've gone over everything on those index cards. We could go back over this part again and again, with different examples, more overlays, more questions; as your perspective changes, the texts will take on new meanings for you. I learn something new every time I teach an Instant Shakespeare workshop, as I hope to communicate in the following Interlude, "More Banging at Swords."

Interlude:
More Banging at Swords:
Encounters at
Shakespeare's Globe,
1981–1997

SAM WANAMAKER, AN accomplished American actor and director, was the charismatic, driving force behind the rebuilding of Shakespeare's Globe. I first met Sam in the summer of 1981.

As a result of my work in Strasbourg, I was asked by the American College in Paris to organize a theatre workshop for the school. The course, which focused on Brecht, included a weekend trip to London to see plays. So that we could continue our acting and directing work while we were there, my longtime friend and colleague Elaine Turner arranged for us to use the Museum of the Shakespearean Stage as our base. This impressive-sounding institution turned out to be a rundown warehouse in Southeast London. There was little in it, especially in the way of heat or light, except a large stuffed bear, a small stage based on the seventeenth-century Cockpit Theatre in Drury Lane, and, of course, Sam Wanamaker.

Over the next decade and a half the Museum would continually reinvent itself. First it became the Bear Gardens Museum, then the International Shakespeare Globe Centre, and now the Globe Education Centre. The bear and the stage are still there. Sam, sadly, is not.

That weekend, though, we used the stage to work scenes and discuss the plays we saw in the evenings. One afternoon, Sam, in a cardigan sweater and flowered shirt from Liberty's, watched our session from the Cockpit balcony. Then he came down, introduced himself to me, and said, "Why don't you come and do this for us? This is where we're going to rebuild Shakespeare's Globe Theatre."

I tried hard to be polite and not too skeptical. But as Sam went on, I found myself agreeing. I couldn't know then that this encounter would change my life and provide me one day with the privilege of working on the Globe stage.

From 1982 to 1991 I ran a summer course at the Globe for American drama students. Each year we recruited eighteen or twenty students for study at the place where the reconstructed Globe would one day stand. Our faculty was drawn from the Royal Academy of Dramatic Art, the London Academy of Music and Dramatic Art, Juilliard, and from among theatre professionals on both sides of the Atlantic. We usually succeeded in mounting a full production at the end of each summer. It was in these workshops, with students from disparate backgrounds and different levels of experience and training, that "Instant Shakespeare" was born.

In 1984, the year a lawsuit was brought by the Southwark Borough Council against the Museum, we couldn't use the Museum and so joined with the British American Drama Academy to offer the course.

The day before our showing of *As You Like It*, the Crown Court found in favor of Sam and the Globe over the rights to the land upon which the theatre would eventually stand. At the last minute we frantically and triumphantly moved our play to the Bear Gardens' stage to celebrate this legal victory with our performance.

The summer of the Royal groundbreaking at the Globe site in 1987 was also the year of the leaking roof. Buckets on the stage gave the prison scenes in *Measure for Measure* an uncanny (no pun intended) realism. In 1990 the Globe was so broke it shut down all but its fund-raising operations; there was no summer course. And in 1992 our summer program was replaced by a course offered through Washington University in St. Louis. I became education director of the Globe's Western Region in 1989 and, later, a member of the executive committee of the Globe's United States board of directors. But those stories—and there are plenty of them— about gaining credibility and funding for the Globe in the United States are somewhat off the subject—"from my text," as Viola says in *Twelfth Night*.

In the summer of 1995, a year and a half after Sam's death, the Globe stage was ready . . . almost. When I arrived in London for the opening events, my heart sank. The temporary stage looked more like a plywood mausoleum than an Elizabethan stage. On opening day the audience was instructed to sit quietly and listen carefully, because the theatre had no roof and no sound system. Worst of all, the actors, some of Britain's best-known, took no notice that this was indeed a theatre without sound, lights, sets, or a roof; that here one could not "act" as if one were at the Barbican or the Olivier, by playing the poetry of Shakespeare's language and not the dynamism of his action. That afternoon I left at intermission, depressed that my idea that Shakespeare at the

Globe would somehow be "different" and vital had not been realized.

The following year I was invited by Hugh Richmond, then the Globe's U.S. education director, to help restage his college production of *Much Ado About Nothing* at the Globe the next summer. The production, to be done by his English students at the University of California at Berkeley, would be fully mounted and serve as the basis for an educational video. I was excited by the opportunity to direct a full production on the Globe stage (and become the first American to do so), but I was also filled with trepidation about what I might find in London.

I would have two weeks, with limited access to the Globe stage, to explore the challenges of the space. I needed to balance the concerns of remounting a college production with the desire to discover as much as possible about the space itself. This would truly be "Instant Shakespeare"! These challenges were, I believed, the very ones that the professional actors had ignored in the previous season.

The Globe, as we found it that summer, and as it has remained, is not an easy stage to work upon. It is simply too big. (Yes, I think they got it wrong!) Unless the pit is absolutely full of groundlings to keep the energy going, the actor's energy dies about three feet from the galleries. I believe that rather than occupying two or three of the exterior bays of the "wooden O," the stage should have been set in front of those bays to produce a smaller circumference.

But this may be nitpicking. As Andrew Gurr, the leading academic scholar on the Globe project has rightly said, the reconstructed Globe is a theatre that Shakespeare himself would feel comfortable working in. Professor Gurr is correct, I believe, if only because of the heightened demand for presence the stage makes on the performer.

According to contemporary accounts, Shakespeare's actors had enormous presence on stage and an abundance of physical energy. In their day they were not so much the equivalent of actors with the Royal Shakespeare Company as they were rock stars playing in Wembly Stadium or Central Park. There was no introspection here, at least not the kind permitted under a spotlight in an enclosed theatre. The introspection required was more along the lines of what one must think about before bungee-jumping off the Golden Gate bridge!

Was it fair to expect these students from U.C. Berkeley, who weren't even drama majors, to fulfill these demands? At Berkeley I had an opportunity to watch the students' performance over the course of a weekend. Done outdoors, in the plaza of an academic building, the production was full of energy and humor. The students did a good job of handling the text; the relationships were clear and the production values stylish. While the audience enjoyed the play, I knew that putting these students on the Globe stage would be a tough test for "Instant Shakespeare."

What to do? In the ten days I had the students in London, they defined their character choices, honed their diction, quickened their timing, and sharpened their physical stamina. But the one thing I emphasized, more than anything else, was the importance of taking responsibility for their choices and actions; of making a commitment to the text and to a character and following it through. I asked them to be specific with their movements, their choice of words, their motivation, their intentions, and the way in which they chose to manifest these actions. I asked them, over and over again, why their character chose to say those particular words, in that particular order, at that particular moment.

But as well as they had handled the "how" of production

(learning the lines, movement, dance, song, etc.), by opening night they had yet to confront the "why" of the characters' specific choices of action, language, and impulse. They had not come to grips with the ultimate question in playing Shakespeare (or any playwright, for that matter) and couldn't see its importance in rehearsal.

As a result, their acting was generic, wallpaper Shakespeare, iambic pentameter Muzak; and I say this in full recognition of the achievement these students made in simply memorizing the lines, getting the text on its feet, and mounting the production as stylishly as they did.

Our performance took place on a lovely English summer evening. About six hundred of our closest friends poured into the theatre—the kids had done a great public relations job in the local pubs and the hostel where they were staying. The Globe management, unprepared for such response, had no small amount of concern. I sat in the third gallery trying hard not to shout out corrections as the performance went along. The first scene was pretty rocky, the cast obviously nervous, and the audience equally anxious. As one young actress put it afterward, "It was soooo scary! I'd never done a play where I didn't know anyone in the audience before."

But by the masque of Act II, things had settled down. The dancing helped burn off the nervous energy, and the play became more focused and much funnier. There was, as is evident in the videotape, enormous warmth in the applause at the end of the production. The audience had enjoyed themselves, and more than that, these kids had done a great job in tackling a major challenge. So why wasn't I happy? I feared that I hadn't succeeded in communicating the essentials of interpretation. The production, I thought, had no presence. There was nothing there that would "linger."

Late the next morning when I arrived at the critique of

the evening's performance (as well as the entire ten days' experience), there was an odd sense of closure for me. I suddenly recalled those very first sessions at the Bear Gardens fifteen years earlier, and my entire history with the Globe seemed strangely telescoped. Finally, it was a reality. We had actually produced a play on the Globe stage—the stage that no one but Sam Wanamaker believed could ever be built.

And in spite of my misgivings about their performance, the residual enthusiasm of these students was too high even for a Grinch like me to dampen. So I began my autopsy of the show by asking a question: If last night were the beginning of our journey, and not the end of it, what would we do next? In other words, if yesterday's performance had been a dress rehearsal or preview, would you have been satisfied with it? The answer, which emerged slowly, surely, and collectively, was "no."

A discussion that was scheduled for half an hour ranged on for two. It was the most important "two hours' traffic" those students had in their entire two weeks. It meant that their experience at the Globe was now at the beginning of their encounter with Shakespeare, not at the end of it. By the end of our discussion, we were left with more questions than answers; questions we would love to solve through more performances. This first encounter with the Globe stage would linger with those students, and with me, all our lives.

It is the unique experience of working near the spot where the Globe once stood that truly changes the scholar, the educator, and the theatre artist. Sam believed it in 1981, and it was still true in 1997. If the Globe is to continue to have a truly international impact, it must become an educational center with opportunities for scholarship and research; it must offer a comprehensive curriculum for actors, directors, teachers, and students of all ages.

Access to the stage, then, who has it and what is done with it, will be central to the Globe's success or failure. The realities of the pressures of access were made abundantly clear to us as we planned educational courses for the opening season. Demands of the professional acting company for a four-play season, continuous guided tours, fund-raising receptions, and public relations functions made another student production or an acting and directing class impossible.

This is why, in 1997, the first official season at the Globe, we chose a "ripple effect" solution by focusing on secondary school teachers. Hugh Richmond and I invited the English-Speaking Union of the United States to join us in sending thirty outstanding American English and drama teachers to London to participate in a workshop called "Teaching Shakespeare Through Performance." The course covered a wide range of topics—scholarship and research, Renaissance music and dance—and featured distinguished lecturers and theatre professionals from both England and America.

What made the course unique and uniquely frustrating was the limited access we had to the Globe stage. Everyone wanted more. There were many questions and not nearly enough time to develop thoughtful answers.

How much of what happens on the Globe stage is relevant to modern theatre? Should it affect contemporary actor training? Is it relevant to what goes on in the classroom? Should it affect teacher training and scholarship? When working on the Globe stage itself, is there a difference between crossing in front of the pillars or behind them? What happens if a chair is placed dead center, upstage, or downstage? How does this affect the actor's relationship with the audience or other actors on stage? Given a monologue or soliloquy, how much of it can be addressed directly to the audience? When do entrances and exits really begin? How much of the action can overlap? What goes on in the balcony? The way the theatre is constructed, can Romeo and Juliet and Antony and Cleopatra really play there?

Some people who have studied with me have accused me of demanding a "right" answer in my work; of questioning them to the point of confusion, or near nervous breakdown. They don't believe me when I say there is no right answer, that chaos is healthy and that, as Brecht was fond of saying, "in contradiction lies our hope." They can't yet hear the false resonance of swords banging in make-believe. But in my own defense I must say that I really do try to keep it simple. For example:

One of the teachers involved in my course was a woman who had taught for many years. She had been a workshop leader in her own right, had written articles and reviews on staging Shakespeare, and was associated with one of the leading Shakespeare-in-the-schools teaching and publishing projects. In other words, she considered herself, and was considered by others, to be something of an expert. When she presented a scene from *A Midsummer Night's Dream*, Act II, scene 1, it went on for exactly four lines before I stopped her and asked her to repeat it.

OBERON: Ill met by moonlight, proud Titania.

TITANIA: What, jealous Oberon? Fairies, skip hence; I have foresworn his bed and company.

OBERON: Tarry, rash wanton. Am I not thy Lord?

Again the same four lines, and again I stopped and asked, "What's wrong with the scene?"

There was some considerable outrage that I hadn't been fair to the teacher or the other actors in the scene, that I hadn't allowed the scene to develop, and that I was looking for a "right" answer. But I insisted, "What's wrong with the scene?"

The teachers were thoroughly frustrated and exasperated. Was it the sexuality? The wantonness? The blocking? The fairies? What!?

"Let's do the scene again," I said, "and this time everyone really watch and listen."

OBERON: Ill met by moonlight, proud Titania.

TITANIA: What, jealous Oberon? Fairies, skip hence; I have foresworn his bed and company.

OBERON: Tarry, rash wanton. Am I not thy Lord?

Finally one of the teachers spoke up. "Why does Oberon say 'tarry' if Titania isn't going anywhere?" Why, indeed? Banging at swords. It's that simple. For Oberon to say "tarry," Titania has to move. She has to. She can't tarry; there are no options. They have to "skip hence." Otherwise it's just so much banging at swords.

Remember that while it may be "hidden in the sand," the truth is always in the text.

PART TWO

Aspects of Performance

· 8 ·

Transitions from Reading to Performance

THE GOAL OF PART ONE is to develop your ability to read a play—aloud or silently—as a "pre-performance" text. It doesn't matter if you are a student, teacher, actor, or director, or what your prior exposure to Shakespeare is. The exercises are structured to have you encounter the texts in a simple, direct, and immediate way. There is no requirement to perform them. I hope you feel that we have succeeded so far.

Part Two is about performance—about transforming those dead texts into living ones. How do we begin this process of transformation, these lessons on performance? As you shall see shortly, this is done by a study of the breath—by literally breathing life back into the plays.

We will start with small, self-contained characters in small, self-contained scenes; characters who exist, fully and completely in order to achieve one thing; characters who want one thing and get it in spite of the obstacles in their paths and the brevity of their scenes. Jean-Louis Barrault, the great French actor best known for his role in the film *Children of Paradise*, wrote similarly of his own training: "Often we played four or five [small parts] in an evening. Take

Richard III. I remember I 'did,' as they say, first a citizen, then Lord Grey and finally a soldier. . . . We explored the smallest, sketchiest part down to its most secret stronghold, its psychological depths."

We'll begin with Marcade from *Love's Labours Lost*, one of my favorite plays. It is the story of young people in love and the foolishness they engage in. (*Antony and Cleopatra*, on the other hand, is about the foolishness older people engage in!) It's about growing up and about youth being wasted on the young. In spite of its arcane and formal verse, its dialogue is among the most fluid and zestful in Shakespeare. If you don't know it, read it and see what you think.

After laboring over love for four and a half acts, the lovers (the young King of Navarre and his courtiers and the Princess of France and her ladies-in-waiting) sit down together to watch a performance put on by the locals, much as the lovers do in *A Midsummer Night's Dream*. As in *Midsummer*, they are having a jolly good time at the locals' expense when Monsieur Marcade, the messenger from the court of the King of France, appears.

Marcade watches the party for a moment, then makes his presence known with the spare dialogue you see below:

MARCADE: God save you, Madame.

PRINCESS: Welcome Marcade, but that thou interrupt'st our merriment.

MARCADE: I am sorry, Madame, for the news I bring is heavy on my tongue. The King your father—

PRINCESS: Dead, for my life.

MARCADE: Even so: My tale is told . . .

PRINCESS: . . . Boyet, prepare. I will away tonight.

All the labors of love have been lost, just like that. These are the only lines Marcade says in the entire play. How do we begin to work on Marcade and his scene?

Use Your *"Frog Overlays"* and *Analyze the Scene*

1. Make the nouns sound like what they mean: *God, Madame, news, tongue, King, father, tale.* Which words or phrases do you feel awkward or uncomfortable saying? "God save you, Madame"? What happens if you omit it? Marcade must stand and wait (and quietly impose his presence on the festivities) until the Princess acknowledges him. She could, but doesn't, begin their dialogue. Why must he? How do you feel about his "Even so"? What happens if you let the silence play those moments for you the first time through?

2. Push the verbs: *save, am, bring, told.* What are Marcade's actions? Let's assume he wants to break the news and get the Princess to leave with him as soon as possible. Does he get what he wants? How?

3. Leave the adjectives and adverbs alone: *sorry, heavy, and so.* There is no need to gild the lily. Play the adjectives and adverbs and see what this does to the delicacy of the scene.

4. Play the "I/thou" relationships: *to whom?* (you, Madame) *about what?* (her father's death). Marcade's relationship to the Princess is made clear through the content of his message and his apparent relationship to the throne. It's clear that everyone, including the young King of Navarre, is watching Marcade and the Princess. That's what gives the scene its tension.

5. Repunctuate for breath. Where are the impulses for

Marcade and the Princess? Even though this is a lightly punctuated scene, you can still remove some of the punctuation marks—the commas in his first two speeches and the dash after "father." Where do the characters breathe?

Now Create Your "Handy Note to Carry Around":

1. What's the end?
2. What's the tune?
3. What's the texture?
4. What's the scene about?

1. What's the end? By the end of the scene, Marcade has delivered his message and the Princess prepares to leave her youthful merrymaking behind. Interestingly, at this point in the Folio text Shakespeare no longer refers to her as Princess but as Queen of France, indicating her elevation to royal responsibility and maturity—a hint to the performer that a change has occurred.

2. What's the tune? "Dead, for my life." Though not stated repeatedly, this line lies beneath every line in the scene and in the spaces between.

3. What's the texture? This is up to you, but consider an example. Everything up to this moment in the play has been light, airy, and summery—a setting for young love. Marcade enters dressed in black. The green of summer turns suddenly frosty and brittle. The first leaf of autumn falls, and a sudden chill sends shivers up everyone's spine.

4. What's the scene about? Growing up and the moment when a person accepts responsibility, and, as in *Hamlet*, mortality. Marcade is the agent of the Princess's maturation. Her love for the young king (see her monologue, "A time me

thinks . . .") will be deeper, richer, and more mature for the experience.

Apply the Shakespeare Paradigm

Why does this particular character say these particular words, at this particular moment, in this particular order? Why is the news "heavy on his tongue," and not "sad in his heart"? Why is his "tale told" and not his "story done"? And so forth.

Play Dead Sea Scrolls

Look carefully at this fragment to see what questions you can answer.

How old is Marcade? Where has he come from? How did he get there? What is his relationship to the Princess? Does he think she's silly? Capable? Who notices Marcade first? Navarre? The Princess? Does Marcade wait like a good courtier for the proper moment to interrupt the party, or does he burst onto the scene because of the urgency of his message? Does he show grief and emotion on his face, or is he stoic, impersonal, and professional?

How does he deliver his first line? Privately? Publicly? When does the Princess sense, know, or guess his message? Before he speaks? During? How does he feel about breaking the news to her at this festive occasion? How does he feel about all those people looking at him? Does it matter? Has he rehearsed his speech?

I answer these questions of performance through the process of "this, not that." I want you to engage in this process from the moment you are cast. Answering these questions prepares you for rehearsal, even if you find new answers once rehearsals begin. This is a way of beginning your creative process. You will start out with multiple answers and eliminate most of them.

Go through the scene from *Love's Labours Lost* again, applying "this, not that" and answering the questions I've posed above. Remember, there are no right or wrong decisions, but you must take responsibility for the ones you make.

· 9 ·

Scenes for Exercises

THE FOLLOWING is a list of scenes for exercises. In them, a character enters, delivers information or makes a request, then leaves. None of the scenes contains any particularly well-known lines or monologues. The scenes are presented in increasing order of complexity and should be worked on before proceeding to the next chapter. Don't do them all at once. Come back to them, again and again, as you've done with the earlier monologue exercises.

Remember, only when you get to the point where you know what the character *wouldn't* do can you begin to understand what he or she *might* do. And when you're finished with these scenes, there are plenty more to be found in the Complete Works of Mr. William Shakespeare.

Merry Wives of Windsor: Act IV, scene 3

Enter HOST *and* BARDOLPH.

BARDOLPH: Sir, the German desires to have three of your horses. The Duke himself will be to-morrow at court, and they are going to meet him.

HOST: What duke should that be comes so secretly? I hear not of him in the court. Let me speak with the gentlemen. They speak English?

BARDOLPH: Ay, sir, I'll call him to you.

HOST: They shall have my horses, but I'll make them pay; I'll sauce them. They have had my house a week at command; I have turned away my other guests. They must come off; I'll sauce them. Come.   *Exeunt.*

Henry VI, Part 2: Act IV, scene 5

Enter LORD SCALES *upon the Tower, walking. Then enter two or three* Citizens *below.*

SCALES: How now! Is Jack Cade slain?

1 CITIZEN: No, my lord, nor likely to be slain; for they have won the bridge, killing all those that withstand them. The Lord Mayor craves aid of your Honour from the Tower to defend the city from the rebels.

SCALES: Such aid as I can spare you shall command;
But I am troubled here with them myself;
The rebels have assay'd to win the Tower.
But get you to Smithfield and gather head,
And thither I will send you Matthew Goffe.
Fight for your king, your country, and your lives;
And so farewell, for I must hence again.   *Exeunt.*

The Winter's Tale: Act III, scene 1

Enter CLEOMENES *and* DION.

CLEOMENES: The climate's delicate, the air most sweet,
Fertile the isle, the temple much surpassing
The common praise it bears.

DION: I shall report,
For most it caught me, the celestial habits
(Methinks I so should term them), and the reverence

Of the grave wearers. O, the sacrifice!
How ceremonious, solemn and unearthly
It was i'th' offering!

CLEOMENES: But of all, the burst
And the ear-deaf'ning voice o'th' Oracle,
Kin to Jove's thunder, so surpris'd my sense
That I was nothing.

DION: If th'event o'th' journey
Prove as successful to the queen,—O be't so!—
As it hath been to us, rare, pleasant, speedy,
The time is worth the use on't.

CLEOMENES: Great Apollo
Turn all to th' best! These proclamations,
So forcing faults upon Hermione,
I little like.

DION: The violent carriage of it
Will clear or end the business: when the Oracle
(Thus by Apollo's great divine seal'd up)
Shall the contents discover, something rare
Even then will rush to knowledge. Go: fresh horses!
And gracious be the issue.   *Exeunt.*

Othello: Act III, scene 4

Enter BIANCA.

BIANCA: Save you, friend Cassio!

CASSIO: What make you from home?
How is't with you, my most fair Bianca?
I'faith, sweet love, I was coming to your house.

BIANCA: And I was going to your lodging, Cassio.

What, keep a week away? seven days and nights?
Eight score eight hours? and lovers' absent hours
More tedious than the dial, eightscore times!
O weary reckoning!

CASSIO: Pardon me, Bianca,
I have this while with leaden thoughts been pressed,
But I shall in a more continuate time
Strike off this score of absence. Sweet Bianca,
[*giving her Desdemona's handkerchief*]
Take me this work out.

BIANCA: O Cassio, whence came this?
This is some token from a newer friend!
To the felt absence now I feel a cause.
Is't come to this? Well, well.

CASSIO: Go to, woman,
Throw your vile guesses in the devil's teeth
From whence you have them! You are jealous now
That this is from some mistress, some remembrance.
No, by my faith, Bianca.

BIANCA: Why, whose is it?

CASSIO: I know not neither, I found it in my chamber.
I like the work well: ere it be demanded,
As like enough it will, I'd have it copied.
Take it, and do't, and leave me for this time.

BIANCA: Leave you? Wherefore?

CASSIO: I do attend here on the general
And think it no addition, nor my wish,
To have him see me womaned.

BIANCA: Why, I pray you?

CASSIO: Not that I love you not.

BIANCA: But that you do not love me.
I pray you, bring me on the way a little,
And say if I shall see you soon at night.

CASSIO: 'Tis but a little way that I can bring you
For I attend here, but I'll see you soon.

BIANCA: 'Tis very good. I must be circumstanced.   *Exeunt.*

Antony and Cleopatra: Act V, scene 2

CLEOPATRA: Hast thou the pretty worm of Nilus there
That kills and pains not?

CLOWN: Truly, I have him; but I would not be the party that
should desire you to touch him, for his biting is immortal.
Those that do die of it do seldom or never recover.

CLEOPATRA: Remember'st thou any that have died on't?

CLOWN: Very many; men and women too. I heard of one of
them no longer than yesterday—a very honest woman,
but something given to lie, as a woman should not do but
in the way of honesty—how she died of the biting of it,
what pains she felt. Truly, she makes a very good report
o'th' worm; but he that will believe all that they say shall
never be saved by half that they do. But this is most falli-
able, the worm's an odd worm.

CLEOPATRA: Get thee hence. Farewell.

CLOWN: I wish you all joy of the worm.
[*Sets down his basket.*]

CLEOPATRA: Farewell.

CLOWN: You must think this, look you, that the worm will do
his kind.

CLEOPATRA: Ay, ay. Farewell.

CLOWN: Look you, the worm is not to be trusted but in the keeping of wise people; for, indeed, there is no goodness in the worm.

CLEOPATRA: Take thou no care; it shall be heeded.

CLOWN: Very good. Give it nothing, I pray you, for it is not worth the feeding.

CLEOPATRA: Will it eat me?

CLOWN: You must not think I am so simple but I know the devil himself will not eat a woman. I know that a woman is a dish for the gods if the devil dress her not. But truly, these same whoreson devils do the gods great harm in their women, for in every ten that they make, the devils mar five.

CLEOPATRA: Well, get thee gone. Farewell.

CLOWN: Yes, forsooth. I wish you joy o'th' worm.   *Exit.*

Extra Credit: The Shopping Bag Assignment

After you've completed all the text work on the scenes above, pick one character from one scene.

Get a large shopping bag and fill it with props, costume pieces, and other items that you believe represent your character, or that your character might use. Don't be literal! Don't put a dagger, crown, and kilt into Macbeth's shopping bag.

Use the shopping bag to manifest the imaginative life of your character. For example, what is Macbeth's favorite food? What does he want served at the banquet? What kind of car does Juliet want her father to buy her when she gets her license? What exactly are the gifts that Hamlet gives to Ophelia? Does she keep them in a little box? Where? If Gertrude's castle were on fire, what would she rush in to rescue? Does she have any pets?

Cut out magazine pictures that give you a sense of the texture of the world the character inhabits. Find swatches of cloth, wood, stones, and shells, anything you can put in your hand to make your character come alive for you. When your shopping bag is full, throw some of the junk out. This is an ongoing process. Sometimes, something you thought was perfect will be eliminated later as your ideas about your character evolve and come into focus. In the end, though, you should be able to step back, empty out the bag, and have a good idea of who this person is.

Out of all the things in your bag, there will be only one or two items that you will actually use on stage. The rest go into making up the hidden life of your character. No one knows they exist but you. On stage, you show only the tip of the iceberg. The rest, as Hamlet says, is silence.

· 10 ·

Aspects of Performance: Breath and Impulse

REMEMBER OUR DEFINITION of acting from Part One?

Acting is the organized and repeatable physical manifestation of an emotional state of being, the corollary to which is: acting is a study of the breath.

No idea can be expressed in performance without the breath. Similarly:

Directing is the concrete organization of manifest behavior into events, the corollary to which is: directing is the study of human relationships.

Impulse generates breath. Isn't that why doctors slap babies' bottoms when they're born? The study of the breath is the study of impulses. Therefore, acting, a study of the breath, is also a study of impulses.

As I have hinted earlier, the language of impulses is pre-verbal. It is the language of wants and needs; of desire and arousal. Having said that, let me try to decode some of this pre-verbal language. Take, for example, the following exchange between King Lear and his youngest daughter, Cordelia, in Act I of *King Lear*.

Lear has created a bidding war among his three daughters for his affections and his estate. The elder two, Goneril and Regan, have proclaimed their love; they have received their dowries and thanked their father. Now it is Cordelia's turn to speak:

LEAR: What can you say to draw
   A third more opulent than your sisters?
   Speak.

CORDELIA: Nothing, my Lord.

LEAR: Nothing?(!)

CORDELIA: Nothing.

LEAR: Nothing will come of nothing. Speak again.

CORDELIA: Unhappy that I am, I cannot heave
   My heart into my mouth.

Remember, we're examining the space between the words, the pre-verbal impulses that lie between what is said and what happens. How long or short are these silences? What happens in them? How palpable is the hurt, the anger, the betrayal? How terrified is Cordelia? Is the punctuation mark after Lear's "Nothing" a question mark or an exclamation point? (Elizabethan compositors often used these two symbols interchangeably.) If it is a question mark, then perhaps Lear is deaf or wants to give Cordelia an opportunity to reconsider her response. If it is an exclamation point, Lear quickly establishes himself as a tyrant.

Previously in this book, whenever I wanted you to read something aloud, I put the text in boldface. Now it is the

margins, the white space between, under, and around the lines, that you should imagine are in bold. Let me give you an analogy that will make those "blank" spaces easier to see.

Spaghetti-Western Shakespeare

Did you ever see one of those Sergio Leone / Clint Eastwood spaghetti Westerns like *The Good, the Bad, and the Ugly,* or *A Fistful of Dollars*? Music, please, complete with solo whistler!

Remember those big close-ups? Those eyes? That squinting? How the long-standing hatred between Eastwood and Eli Wallach was encapsulated in those close-ups? How long or short were the silences? What happened in them? How palpable was the hurt, anger, and betrayal between them—all without a line of dialogue? How terrified is Clint—or Cordelia? That's the language between the words that I'm talking about. **Be bold** and try this:

Take the Lear/Cordelia scene and play it at "high noon" on the streets of Laredo in extreme close-up. Go ahead. Make my day.

LEAR: What can you say to draw
    A third more opulent than your sisters?
    Speak.

Squinty-eyed exchange between father and daughter.

CORDELIA: Nothing, my Lord.

Reactions from the townspeople. Some of them run to the saloon for cover.

LEAR: Nothing?

The old man squints tighter, his finger itching at the trigger.

CORDELIA: Nothing.

She is cool, fearless. Somewhere a horse whinnies.

LEAR: Nothing will come of nothing. Speak again.

He laughs mockingly and spits cigar juice from the side of his mouth.

CORDELIA: Unhappy that I am, I cannot heave
    My heart into my mouth.

Silence . . . and then, suddenly, a hail of iambic pentameter gunfire explodes between them!

    Do you see how much can be contained in the margin, the silence, the space between the lines?

The Space Between the Lines

Read the Lear/Cordelia dialogue aloud four times. The first time, read it without pauses and overlap the lines; the second time, impose a count of three between each exchange; the third time, a count of five; and finally, a count of seven.

LEAR: What can you say to draw
    A third more opulent than your sisters?
    Speak (.)

CORDELIA: Nothing, my Lord (.)

LEAR: Nothing (?/!)

CORDELIA: Nothing (.)

LEAR: Nothing will come of nothing. Speak again (.)

CORDELIA: Unhappy that I am (,) I cannot heave ()
    My heart into my mouth (.)

Do you see how the length of the silences changes the relationship between father and daughter, sovereign and subject? Remember, there is no right and wrong here, just the exploration of the margins. Lear and Cordelia can rage back and forth at one another; they can be pensive, shy, or hesitant. They can overlap their lines or suffer in silence. Whatever happens between the words will change the meaning of the scene.

Now you see why I said earlier that the language is the least important thing in Shakespeare. The study of the impulse that precedes language, the breath, is the key to performance.

Nothing in the texts, in Shakespeare's language, will help you determine how to play the silences. This "space between the lines" is what the French Symbolist poets called "les blancs," literally the white space between the letters, the abyss in which all significant speech originates. In the silences lies what Antonin Artaud, the French actor, director, and founder of the Theatre of Cruelty, called the "meta-language" of the theatre, the meaning beyond language. This is what Peter Brook means when he speaks of the theatre's unique ability to make "the invisible, visible."

Now that we have the margin and the impulse, what do we do? We breathe. Let's look at Lear and Cordelia again. Everything we know about them is expressed through their breath:

HE: Nothing?

What's his reaction? Shock? Anger? Is he hard of hearing?

SHE: Nothing.

What's going through her head? What's happening to her heartbeat? Are her palms sweaty, her face flushed?

HE: Nothing will come of nothing.

Is this advice? A threat? A warning? An old proverb? How long do we wait here?

HE: Speak again.

Is it an invitation, a second chance, or a command? All this is implied from a study of the breath.

Inspiration / Expiration

Shakespeare, like most good writers of dialogue, constructed his lines for the actor's breath. The actor breathes every time a new idea comes into his head. That's why it's called inspiration!

Remember those cartoon drawings where the character gets an idea, a light bulb goes on over his head, and he gasps an intake of breath? "Aha!" he says. Inspiration! Then, on the next breath, the expiration, the character acts on his idea. Inspiration and expiration must be constantly renewed or we die.

The goal of this "idea breathing" is to make the transition from two-dimensional texts to three-dimensional events. Working with "idea breathing" establishes a strong connection between the longer breath and the longer line, the longer line and the larger idea. No one thinks, acts, or speaks word by word. If they did, would you want to listen to them for two hours? The opposite error occurs when an actor doesn't fully understand what he or she is saying, and instead plays a pattern of sound. To break this pattern you must stop, re-think, and breathe before you can continue. The physical exercises coming up are geared to help you do just that.

Some directors and teachers believe that if you strictly follow the punctuation, spelling, and capitalization found in the First Folio of 1623, you will achieve Shakespeare's intentions for what to stress and where to breathe. But the First Folio, the collection of Shakespeare's plays published by his friends after his death, although a crucial and essential reference work, is just that, a reference work.

The Elizabethan printers who first published Shakespeare's plays thought it fully within their rights to repunctuate texts. They usually added rather than deleted punctuation. Even in the earliest editions of the plays, the punctuation, and therefore the meaning, has been somewhat altered. The Folio text of *Hamlet*, for example, is much more heavily punctuated than either the First or Second Quarto editions; relatively light commas are turned into colons or exclamation marks.

I am suggesting that when it comes to the breath, your instincts are as valid as anyone else's, if you do your homework! As you refine your work, there will be plenty of opportunities to use the Folio and Quarto texts as well as modern scholarly editions as references in your creative process. But now is the time for you to breathe and **be bold!**

Cycles of Performance

No idea can be expressed in performance without the breath. The ephemeral in theatre occurs only when human beings breathe in the same venue; when actor and audience, enclosed within the theatre's three-dimensional volume, share this breath and exchange impulse and energy in what I call a cycle of performance.

At the beginning of the cycle, I, as a reader, encounter Shakespeare as a two-dimensional piece of literature. Then I transform that text into a three-dimensional event as I "make it my own" in rehearsals; I also transform myself from reader to performer. Ultimately the audience gains its understanding of the text through my performance. The cycle of performance becomes complete when, in the best of all possible worlds, the audience is inspired (that word again) to have its own encounter with Shakespeare. (Audiences should leave the theatre wanting more Shakespeare, not less!)

Every time I direct a play, I outline this cycle for myself, as a reminder of my responsibility to create in performance a meeting between the author and the audience. The diagram looks something like this:

Author/Text/Reader . . . Reader/Text/Performer . . .
Performer/Text/Audience . . . Audience/Text/Author

If I fail to come to grips with the text in my pre-performance reading, if the text does not get across in performance, and if the audience is not transformed or allowed to have its own encounter with the author, there is no cycle of performance and therefore no theatrical event. Those productions that achieve part of this cycle may be entertaining, informative, even stunning and moving, but they are not what I believe the theatre is ultimately about.

· 11 ·

Aspects of Performance: A Practical Study of the Breath

AS I SAID IN THE PRECEDING CHAPTER, acting is a study of the breath. But I cannot teach you to breathe with this book.

No book can do that. Even a good acting, yoga, voice, or singing teacher can't "teach" you to breathe. We may give you exercises, lessons, and mantras, but I've come to believe that every individual breathes differently; that the programming of breath and impulses in the body is different for each of us. Some solutions work for some people and others do not.

Breathing makes you vulnerable. Most of the time in the "real" world, we don't want to be vulnerable; we need all the protection we can get at work, in our relationships, on the freeway, or at the checkout counter. But in performance we need to allow ourselves to be vulnerable, to breathe and not edit ourselves, to involve our entire organism in the creative process, not just our heads. That's why we need a friend. And the floor is your friend!

The Floor Is Your Friend

Nothing is scarier for actors than to be up on their two feet in rehearsal, class, or even their own living rooms, trying to breathe, say the words, and explore the spaces between the lines.

Acting, like being in love, is a very scary activity. You wonder if you'll be liked, wanted, and accepted. You worry about your performance and your breath. You don't know what to say. You're afraid you're not pretty enough, thin enough, tall enough, and all the rest. That's why, in acting, you need to remember that the floor is your friend. You can throw up on it, fall down on it, stomp on it, and make an ass of yourself on it, and it will not (Southern California earthquakes excepted) abandon you. Most important, it will hold you up.

I'm not kidding here. The floor is your friend. This is very important. It will hold you up. You have no responsibility for gravity or the laws of physics while you act. Too many actors spend too much energy holding themselves and their tensions up while on stage. Acting is a lonely and frightening business most of the time; you often feel as if everyone is watching and judging you, and they probably are. It's nice to know that, if nothing else, the floor is your friend.

Go on, say it. It will make you feel better: **The floor is your friend.**

Like amphibians, we crawled through the primordial ooze before we walked. On a primal, pre-Jungian level, in the deepest part of the brain, there is an inherent fear that these two flat things called feet won't hold us up. As the earth spins through the solar system, we would much rather be curled up in the fetal position!

Actor Defies Gravity, Film at Eleven!

Here's a simple deep-breathing exercise:

Lie on the floor, preferably one that isn't carpeted. (You might want to put a towel underneath you.) Stretch your arms out to the sides with your palms down and your fingertips touching the floor. Now breathe. Just breathe. Breathe along the spine, the small of the back, under your tush, down to your knees, under your ankles, over your toes, right back over your legs, crotch, stomach, chest, shoulders, arms, neck and head, and back down again. Keep going. Keep breathing.

Don't bite your lip as people often do when they try to breathe! After a while you should feel all your weight sink into the floor while the tips of your fingers gently vibrate from the breath. After a couple of minutes of breathing this way, get up . . . slowly. Your head and shoulders should be the last things up! They won't fall off. If you feel dizzy, lie back down and breathe. Remember, the floor is your friend.

You are making an historic transition here, one our ancestors made millions of years ago. All of your weight—the organs, muscles, and bones that felt so comfortable and secure on the floor—now must get up on those little feet. Go on. Try it. Breathe. Don't think! Keep breathing. Take your time now and enjoy your breath. Don't bite your lip. Breathe.

Stimulus / Impulse / Response

One of the main differences between European and American theatre concerns the approach to acting. European actors—especially those in Eastern Europe where roles are still memorized and learned like opera repertory—like to do "things" ("trucs" the French call them) to demonstrate the cleverness of their interpretation, their skill as actors, and the vision of the director. For modern Japanese actors, trained in a theatre where form is still everything, breaking the frame of these "trucs" to find a sense of realism is the greatest challenge.

To us, acting means responding, reacting, being—not executing pre-planned moves and maneuvers. You did enough thinking in the pre-performance (analytical and reading) phase of your work. You cannot think and act at the same time. Nobody wants to see you straining and sweating on stage as you "act." Acting sucks!

Go ahead, say it: **Acting sucks!**

I say it in my workshops and rehearsals. If you are conscious of your "acting" while performing, you cannot possibly "be"; you can't breathe. Tension-filled acting, which only appears to be dynamic, is really for amateurs. It forces you to hold a pose for the entire life of a character. Nothing can or ever will surprise you on stage. Acting sucks!

People hold themselves up defensively—by their shoulders, chest, knees, or neck—in response to a threatening situation. This puts enormous tension into those areas, much of which we carry with us all our lives. Reichian therapists call this "armor," and we start developing it as children. It blocks the organism's (your) ability to respond to stimuli. It stops the flow of impulses through the body, stops the flow of breath, stops communication. Without communication there is no theatrical event.

Acting takes enormous physical energy, but no one wants to see you huff and puff, strained and tense, through a performance. We want you to look elegant and at ease in your role. Relax, breathe, and trust in your body, your self, the floor, and your partner. Trust that who you are and what you are doing are interesting and appreciated.

Bifurcation

When we attempt to think and act at the same time, we become bifurcated—split in two, going in two directions at once.

Actors are among the most bifurcated people in the world; they constantly monitor themselves. Was I good enough in this scene? Did I demonstrate enough passion, anger, emotion? Was I clear enough? Did I say the words correctly? Did I get all the consonants, the punctuation, the capitalization, the emotion, and meaning? Did I get the imagery right? The footnotes? The subtext? The private moments?

The Quick Fix

So what can we do about bifurcation? We can apply the quick fix!

As I've already mentioned, it is not the province of this book to teach you how to breathe. There are many ways to learn to breathe—Alexander technique; the techniques of Kristin Linklater and Patsy Rodenburg; martial arts; yoga; singing; swimming, etc. All these methods require long study, concentration, and commitment to the gradual evolution of your self, body, awareness, and breath.

But time is sometimes a luxury we cannot afford in the theatre. As a director and an acting teacher I found the need to develop physical exercises that would demonstrate instantly the difference between what an actor was doing and what I, as director, wanted in a scene.

These exercises are "quick fixes." They are prescriptive, like aspirin, and not diagnostic. Take a couple and you won't be cured, but you'll get through rehearsal. It's essential that you keep this in mind as you proceed with them. They are not a replacement for detailed, patient work on the voice, breath, and self, but they are useful for momentarily unblocking the body so that the impulse and breath can be released. Use them in rehearsal or class when you are "stuck."

To do these, you will need to memorize a monologue. (You may have already committed several to memory in the "frog overlay" process.) Don't perform the monologue; just say the words, breathe, and do the exercises.

When you do the following push-ups, jackknifes, or shoulder stands while reciting "To be or not to be," the organism is pushed toward an extreme state of bifurcation. Finally the body takes over, reprograms itself as a single unit, and says, "Hey, you know what? If I ease up here, breathe, and work efficiently as a unified organism, I can get through this!"

Remember that in order to perform, actors and actresses must be in good physical condition. These exercises require strength, stamina, and flexibility. Use common sense and an honest appraisal of your capabilities when doing them. After you have become familiar with all of them, choose the ones that work best for you and use them when you need to.

The exercises are not listed in any particular order.

PUSH-UPS

Do four or five push-ups, then begin the monologue. Continue doing push-ups until you get through the entire monologue. Stop. Collapse onto the floor. The floor is your friend!

Begin again. Do four or five more push-ups (no monologue this time). Stand up and say your monologue. Be careful not to hold your breath or bite your lip.

You'll often find that you will forget the monologue as

you say it during the exercises. This indicates that you have memorized a pattern of sound and failed to understand the impulses under the text. You have forgotten that pattern, and the body is reprogramming itself for new impulses. Concentrate on getting through the exercise. Your body is working more efficiently now to achieve its goal of getting through the monologue. Let it.

SHAKE OUT THE WRISTS
Stand up and shake out your wrists as you say the monologue. Keep your hands out in front of you, down by your sides, or stretched out to the sides. Doing this creates a field of kinetic resistance that you must play through.

JACKKNIFE
Lie flat on your back on the floor. (It's your friend, remember.) With your arms stretched straight back over your head, jackknife forward, take a quick, deep breath, and sit up, keeping your arms and legs straight. Grab your ankles in mid-air (or as close as you can come). Be careful not to sit on the bottom of your spine. Keep breathing and don't bite your lip. Maintain your balance while sitting. Release and gently extend your arms out to your sides. Then bring your head and back down to the floor. Keep breathing. When your head and shoulders have touched the floor, slowly lower your legs to the floor. Release all your tension into the floor.

Try this three or four times without saying the monologue. Just practice breathing, jackknifing up, balancing, holding the ankles, releasing, and coming down. You'll notice that once you begin lowering your legs, you'll get a "glitch" in your stomach muscles, especially if you are breathing through the entire movement! It will be at that point that you will want to let everything go and simply drop to the floor. It's the bifurcated body telling you, "Hey, this is nuts!"

Breathe through that moment and continue the jackknife until you are flat on the floor. Now do the jackknife again and start the monologue, balancing yourself while holding your ankles. Release and come down. You'll know when you've hit that "glitch" because the words just won't want to come out. Your body is working against itself as you strain your neck, chest, arm, and leg muscles to complete a monologue for which they are not needed!

Relax. Keep breathing and finish the monologue as you sink into the floor. After you've done this three or four times, you may want to turn on your side and curl up in the fetal position in order to stretch your back.

SHOULDER STAND

You may want to try this two or three times without the monologue to get the hang of it.

Lie on your back, then roll gently into a ball by wrapping your arms around your knees and tucking your head down so that your forehead touches your knees. Roll forward until your momentum carries you up onto your shoulders. Support yourself by bringing your hands to the small of the back and, if necessary, your elbows to the floor behind you. Stretch your legs straight out behind you so that your knees are over your head and your toes touch the floor behind you (or as close as they will come).

Breathe. Bring your legs straight up and breathe until you feel balanced. Now begin the monologue. Keeping your legs straight, bring your toes back down over your head until they come to the floor behind you again. Then, still keeping the legs straight, lower your bottom to the floor. Keep breathing and don't bite your lip. Lower your legs (keep them straight!) the rest of the way to the floor.

Somewhere in there you will find that "glitch" again in your stomach. It's a key signal. Keep breathing until your legs slowly reach the floor. Collapse into the floor. Remember, the floor is your friend.

The more you breathe, the more you control the exercise. You'll find less tension in your legs and other parts of the body which are not involved in the exercise. Gravity will do nicely, thank you. Trust physics.

REPEAT THE SLOW BREATHING EXERCISE ON THE FLOOR
Stand up slowly, allowing your head and shoulders to be the last things up. When you are about halfway up, that is, with your legs straight, but doubled over at the waist and head hanging loosely near your knees, put your hands on the "spongy" part of the small of your back (over the kidneys). Now breathe. Feel the breath move your hands. Keep breathing.

Come up slowly, making sure you continue to feel the breath through the small of your back. Keep your head and neck loose. (They won't fall off.) Your head should be the last thing up. Keep your hands on the small of your back to check your breathing. Keep breathing. Say your monologue.

JAW EXERCISE
This is a little messy, but very useful. Stand up and open your mouth wide. Put your first two fingers into your mouth just over your lower teeth. Gently pull down. (The jaw extends all the way to the ears, and you should feel it connected there.)

Gently let the weight of your arm pull your jaw down. Now do your monologue, keeping your jaw down. (Don't worry about diction!) When you finish, stretch your face back and open, as if you were making a silent scream, then pucker up and "scrunch" it tight, as if you've just tasted something very sour. Gently shake your head out, from side to side, making "motor boat" noises as you do. Then stop, breathe, and say the monologue.

THE OBSCENE PHONE CALL

Put your fingers gently on your sternum. Breathe. Keep your jaw loose and lips apart. On a soft "ha" syllable, breathe as if you are making an obscene phone call. This is also the sound you make when the doctor puts a stethoscope on your chest and tells you to "breathe."

You should feel the vibrations of your sternum on the tips of your fingers. (If you don't, you are probably producing the sound in your throat, from the vocal cords.) Relax, breathe, bring your shoulders to your ears, and let them drop with a big sigh of resignation ("ah, me!"). Then, on the next breath, with your fingers still on your chest, imagine yourself moving your fingers off the chest with the breath. Go easy. This is a gentle exercise—a good one to do when you are tired.

When you have a more or less consistent "ha" on each breath, say the monologue, taking a breath wherever you need to, as if you are making an obscene phone call. Remember, just a few words at a time on each breath is fine. Don't push—the sound needs to go only as far as the telephone in front of you. Keep breathing.

WAITING ROOM TERROR

This is a good one to do when you're waiting for an audition or sitting in class waiting to perform your monologue.

Sit in a chair with your hands loosely on your lap and your feet flat on the floor. Beginning with your toes, tense up every muscle in your body, one at a time: toes, soles of the feet, ankles, calves, thighs, hips, waist, stomach, chest, shoulders, neck, chin, lips, forehead, scalp, arms, elbows, hands, and fingers. Hold the tension for a three count *without breathing*. Then, beginning with the fingers, breathe and release the muscles in reverse order, until you return to your toes.

Relax, breathe, and say the monologue silently to yourself. Then stand up and say it. Do you see how much effort it takes to be tense and nervous? And how much more the body enjoys being relaxed and open? (It also freaks out the competition waiting in the room with you!)

Okay now, off you go. But remember, doing a few push-ups, shaking out your wrists, or hanging on to your jaw does not—repeat, not!—replace a long, slow, detailed study of the breath. Having said that, do you notice the one thing these exercises have in common? They are all tactile. Your hands are on your back, your chest, or your jaw. Your shoulders, spine, or buttocks are on the floor. You get physical feedback from the floor and movements of your own body that you can process without having to think. If you're still "stuck," it means you're probably doing too much thinking and self-monitoring. Stop monitoring yourself and get the thermometer out!

Getting the Thermometer Out

In the old days, babies' temperatures were taken rectally. Now we have fancy thermometers that are put into the baby's ear. I'm sure this makes the baby happier, but it's a less effective image for what I want to convey. You cannot be present in your work and at the same time continually monitor yourself by taking your own emotional temperature. Get the thermometer out! I know it's a bit vulgar, but saying it will make you feel much better. Believe me.

Get the thermometer out! If you're busy watching yourself, then you're "acting," and we all know that *acting sucks!*

An actor or actress is like an organism under a microscope. Everyone is watching you, so you don't need to. You can't move forward in your life and work if you are constantly taking your own temperature. Continual self-monitoring guarantees failure and nervous breakdowns. *Get the thermometer out!*

Like that bifurcated organism under a microscope, an actor on stage and a character in a play responds to a stimulus. Your impulses, and the responses they generate, can be simple, direct, and immediate. You can work efficiently and confidently without monitoring or editing yourself, without hiding behind your armor. You don't want to be bifurcated, do you? Of course not!

Do your homework; be as prepared as you can be about what you want to say and why you want to say it. If people like what you are doing, terrific, if not . . . well, they can go jump in the lake, to put it politely.

In our daily lives, we negotiate our way, trying not to offend anyone, trying to be inclusive, nonjudgmental, accepting, approving, supportive, and sensitive. The great thing about Shakespeare's characters is how simple, direct, and immediate they are—even Hamlet.

Shakespeare Direct

In *Much Ado About Nothing*, for example, Beatrice tells Benedick to "Kill Claudio!" She does not say, "Gee, I'm terribly conflicted about this, and you might think me less of a person, but do you think it would be too much to ask if I were to suggest that you might possibly terminate the existence of the non-gender-specific significant other who possibly may have transgressed on the personal space of a relative of mine?"

I'm not making this up. I once saw a production in the San Francisco area in which Beatrice played the line just as I have described it—very politically correct. Needless to say, there were no "sparks" in her relationship with Benedick; at this crucial point in the play, nothing was at risk between them. They were very nice, very civilized to each other, but nothing happened—no relationship, no action, no event. They played the footnotes to the scene, not the scene itself.

Keep it simple. This is what Brecht meant when he said that theatre should be approached "naively." Let somebody else write the footnotes. Follow what David Mamet calls the KISS rule—Keep It Simple, Stupid.

You are making a big transition to performance here. If you find that you are making life miserable for yourself and everyone around you, in what should be a joyous process of "re-creation," just do a few push-ups and get on with it. Speaking out loud, tell your bifurcated self:

1. **The floor is your friend!**
2. **Acting sucks!**
3. **Get the thermometer out!**
4. **Keep it simple, Stupid!**

Chapter Exercise

Return to the monologues in Chapter 4. Go through them again using the "quick fix" exercises. Keep the work simple, direct, and immediate. Keep breathing and, most of all, remember, the floor is your friend!

· 12 ·

Isabella's Voice

AS WE WORK TOWARD the interpretation and performance of complete roles and texts, I want to place the Shakespeare Paradigm in a larger context—that of distinguishing the individual voice of a given Shakespearean character from that of any other Shakespearean character.

One of the reasons I dislike Shakespeare scene study is the tendency of scenes taken out of context to sound alike. Why should Hamlet sound like Lear or Macbeth, or Rosalind like Julia or Viola? All too often these characters simply sound "Shakespearean" in a generally tragic, heroic, or comic way. How can we avoid this "wallpaper Shakespeare"? Let's play some "Dead Sea Scrolls."

Portia and Isabella: Fragments of Mercy

Both Isabella in *Measure for Measure* and Portia in *The Merchant of Venice* plead for mercy on behalf of a loved one. The women have many similarities; they are both single and virginal, parentless, and on their own in a man's world; they are both objects of desire, about the same age, and from the same well-to-do merchant class.

Both are clever, intelligent, and capable women. Both

take initiatives crucial to the outcome of the play: Isabella asks her brother to sacrifice his life for her chastity; Portia strides into the Venetian court to rescue the merchant. Both dress up to disguise their sexuality—one as a nun, the other as a young man. And both ultimately depend upon men to achieve their objectives.

There are, of course, significant differences between the women. Isabella is a novice nun, and Portia would like, perhaps, to marry. Isabella is Viennese; Portia is a Venetian. Portia speaks publicly about mercy in the trial scene of Act IV while Isabella does it privately in the "judge's chambers" of Act II. Examined in just these fragments, are there enough similarities in their speeches to allow us to view Isabella and Portia interchangeably?

For example, both women compare mercy to kingly attributes of crown, sceptre, sword, and truncheon:

PORTIA: The quality of mercy is not strained;
    It droppeth as the gentle rain from heaven
    Upon the place beneath. It is twice blest:
    It blesseth him that gives, and him that takes.
    'Tis mightiest in the mightiest. It becomes
    The thronèd monarch better than his crown;
    His sceptre shows the force of temporal power,
    The attribute to awe and majesty
    Wherein doth sit the dread and fear of kings;
    But mercy is above this sceptre'd sway.
    It is enthroned in the hearts of kings;
    It is an attribute to God himself,
    And earthly power doth then show likest God's
    When mercy seasons justice. . . .

ISABELLA: Too late? Why, no; I that do speak a word
    May call it back again. Well, believe this:

No ceremony that to great ones 'longs,
Not the king's crown, nor the deputed sword,
The marshall's truncheon, nor the judge's robe
Become them with one half so good a grace
As mercy does.
If he had been as you, and you as he,
You would have slipped like him; but he, like you,
Would not have been so stern.

Even if their language is similar, I believe their voices are distinct. How do we manifest this?

Read through both scenes—Act IV, scene 1 of *Merchant*, and Act II, scene 2 of *Measure*. When you get to the appropriate point in each scene, swap the monologues. In other words, after Angelo tells Isabella, "He's sentenced; 'tis too late," she replies with Portia's answer:

Too late? Why no:

The quality of mercy is not strained.
It droppeth as the gentle rain from heaven
Upon the place beneath. It is twice blest:
It blesseth him that gives, and him that takes.
'Tis mightiest in the mightiest. It becomes
The thron'ed monarch better than his crown;
His sceptre shows the force of temporal power,
The attribute to awe and majesty
Wherein doth sit the dread and fear of kings;
But mercy is above this sceptre'd sway.
It is enthroned in the hearts of kings;
It is an attribute to God himself,
And earthly power doth then show likest God's
When mercy seasons justice. . . .

And after Shylock says, "On what compulsion must I? Tell me that?," Portia replies with Isabella's words:

> Well, believe this:
> No ceremony that to great ones 'longs,
> Not the king's crown, nor the deputed sword,
> The marshall's truncheon, nor the judge's robe
> Become them with one half so good a grace
> As mercy does.
> If he had been as you, and you as he,
> You would have slipped like him; but he, like you,
> Would not have been so stern.

The scenes come to a crashing halt when you make these transpositions. Even if one actress played both roles in repertory, the voices of Isabella and Portia are unique. They are specific and nontransferable because *voice is the manifestation of character-in-action.*

Impulse-Voice-Action

Voice is the *process* of character-in-action, and voice is the *essence* of character-in-action.

You can take away a character's words, but you can't take away a character's voice. Before Juliet urges the steeds to gallop, she has an image of them that compels her to use exactly those words to describe what she sees and feels.

We create character through this process of impulse-to-language-to-voice. Voice—how things are said—is a function of language—what is said. Language is a function of impulse—what we want and need to say. Performance is the culmination of impulse, language, and action—an event which manifests relationships on stage.

Part of "this, not that" is the elimination of what Isabella (or Lear or Juliet) *doesn't* want, the "voices" she will not use. Her voice is the essence of her identity, and identity is always in a state of self-actualization, growing, and becoming. Character is dynamic, not static; it changes, moves toward its ultimate goal and root-action, and learns from the choices it makes along the way.

Let's look at Isabella's voice again, this time in Act V. What kind of justice does she want? Does she seek the same justice in Acts I and II that she wants here? Only in the last scene does a principal theme (what the play is about) become clear: justice is not as "measurably" black and white as an "Angelo for a Claudio; death for death." As the Duke measures out justice for Isabella, he asks her to have mercy on Angelo. This event forces her to confront and change her conception of justice; it forces her to confront her image of herself. This is why she is reduced to silence at the end of the play. But even silence is an aspect of her "voice." How does she come to it?

Isabella's Voice

At the beginning of *Measure for Measure*, Isabella is a novice nun urged to come out of her convent in order to plead for her brother's life. She begins hesitantly, but as the stakes increase she becomes more and more articulate and passionate (some would say fanatical). In the last scene of the play, however, after she pleads for mercy for Angelo, the man who has tried to seduce her and execute her brother, she says absolutely nothing.

In what may be one of Shakespeare's most ambiguous theatrical moments, she remains utterly silent as the Duke, her secret admirer for much of the play, offers her his hand in marriage. There is no indication in the text that she wants, expects, or even accepts his proposal. But, given the world of the play and the playwright, it is probable that she does. If so, how willing is she suddenly to become the Duke's bride, and not, as a nun, a chaste bride of Christ? Does the Duke merely occupy a more powerful position of seduction, or is there real love between them, a "marriage of true minds"?

This last scene, moreover, is an excellent example of Fergusson's "histrionic sensibility." Its focus, even as the Duke measures out his justice, is on the silent Isabella. The scene succeeds only if her three-dimensional presence is held firmly in the forefront of the audience's mind. To accomplish this, we must clearly establish her voice throughout the course of the play. It is a powerful voice, especially when silent.

Let's look at more "Dead Sea Scroll" fragments to see how that voice develops.

FRIAR: Now is your time. Speak loud, and kneel before him.

ISABELLA: (*kneeling*) O royal Duke! Vail your regard
Upon a wronged—I would fain have said, a maid.
O worthy prince, dishonor not your eye
By throwing it on any other object,
Till you have heard me in my true complaint,
And given me justice, justice, justice, justice!

The interesting thing in this fragment is the repetition of the word "justice." Why isn't one enough? Why not just two or three? Why (other than to fill out the meter) must Isabella call four times for justice?

There are many possible answers, and the "right or wrong" of the scene cannot be determined without reference to the rest of the play. But suppose, in our Dead Sea digging, we find a fragment, one from another play, *King Lear*:

LEAR: Howl, howl, howl, howl! O, you are men of stones.
    Had I your tongues and eyes, I'd use them so
    That heaven's vault should crack. She's gone for ever.
    I know when one is dead and when one lives.
    She's dead as earth. . . .

Here is another four-word repetition on "howl." Is Lear howling or commanding others to howl? Why is he howling? Focus on the fragments "histrionically." Repeat them, say them, and play with them for a while. What happens to you as you do?

Howl, howl, howl, howl!

Remember, we don't know that Lear has spent most of the past night howling at nature and his daughters. Now:

Justice, justice, justice, justice!

Again, we do not know that Isabella's earlier idea of "justice" included giving her chastity a moral value equal to her brother's life. Let's add another fragment.

Howl, howl, howl, howl! O, you are men . . .

O royal Duke! . . . Justice, justice, justice, justice!

An old man and a young woman plead with "men" plural and one "royal Duke." Even the function and sound of the "O"s are different. After the "howls," "O, you are men" contains a shuddering release of emotion. "O royal Duke!" before "justices" is a springboard to get the Duke's attention. But are we any closer to finding Isabella's "voice"? Try this: substitute the "howls" for "justice" and vice versa.

ISABELLA: (*kneeling*) O royal Duke! Vail your regard
    Upon a wronged—I would fain have said, a maid.

O worthy prince, dishonor not your eye
By throwing it on any other object,
Till you have heard me in my true complaint,
And howl, howl, howl, howl!

LEAR: Justice, justice, justice, justice!
. . . O, you are men of stones.
Had I your tongues and eyes, I'd use them so
That heaven's vault should crack. She's gone for ever.
I know when one is dead and when one lives.
She's dead as earth. . . .

The speeches almost work on the level of sound, rhythm, sense, and meaning, and yet, on the level of voice they do not. They fail an analysis of "why a particular character says a particular word at a particular moment."

Isabella is not wild or irrational; she is specific, precise, what we might even call "up-tight." She weighs her chastity against her brother's life; she weighs her justice against Marianna's pleas for mercy.

MARIANNA: Sweet Isabel, take my part;
Lend me your knees, and all my life to come
I'll lend you all my life to do you service.

DUKE: Against all sense you do importune her.
. . . He dies for Claudio's death.

ISABELLA: (*kneeling*) Most bounteous, sir.
Look, if it please you, on this man condemned
As if my brother lived. . . . For Angelo,
His act did not o'ertake his bad intent,
And must be buried but as intent
That perished by the way. Thoughts are no subjects,
Intents but merely thoughts.

MARIANNA: Merely, my lord.

DUKE: Your suit's unprofitable. Stand up, I say. . . .

The key to Isabella's voice lies in her silent kneeling. That action brings her to a "boundary situation," a moment when her entire system of values, everything she holds dear and important, is challenged and threatened. In this, like all boundary situations, a character is presented with a clear if ultimate choice: adapt or die.

Isabella's voice is trembling at this moment from the inner struggle between her contempt for Angelo and her Christian devotion to mercy and goodness. It may shatter her. How she kneels, when she kneels, why she kneels, and the myriad questions contained in that moment are critical to understanding her character.

In his production of Jean-Claude Carriere's brilliant translation, *Mesure pour mesure*, Peter Brook allowed the actress playing Isabella as much time as she needed each night to make that decision. It was her life on the line at that moment. Nothing less. The silence—sometimes as long as five minutes—was riveting. It spoke as loudly as all the words Shakespeare wrote.

Remember that Shakespeare's characters are not fixed entities from beginning to end. Hamlet, Macbeth, and Isabella change, grow, and develop as a result of what happens to them in the course of the play. At the heart of the acting problem is this question: how do we make these icons, whom we know so well, live *as if* we were seeing them for the first time?

Voice and Essence

In the margins between Isabella's words, her impulses, and her action, a breath rises in the actress's throat. That breath will support the impulse and its manifestation and give Isabella her voice. Remember: acting is a study of the breath.

Isabella's voice can belong only to her. Our job, as performers and interpreters re-creating Isabella (or Lear, or Hamlet), is not to impose our opinion of Isabella on her voice, but to allow Isabella to speak. We must reveal the voice of the author, not impose the voice of the agent.

We accomplish this in the theatre, particularly in Shakespeare, through rigorous analysis of the text, intimate exploration of our characters and ourselves, and a commitment to the possibility of presence in performance. We watch for what is "hidden in the sand" of Isabella's character. This insistence on allowing the characters to speak with and in their own voices is the reason for the Shakespeare Paradigm: why does this particular character say these particular words, at this particular moment, in this particular order?

This, as I said at the beginning, is why Hamlet must say "am I" and not "I am"; why Macbeth must say "foul and fair" rather than "fair and foul." To change the specific, the particular choice of words changes the voice of the character, and hence the voice of the playwright.

Let me give you one last example. Here are Isabella's brother Claudio and Hamlet on the subject of death—a region of ice, an "unknown region," from which no traveler returns. Their images are similar, but their voices are unique. Our job is to let each one speak:

CLAUDIO: Ay, but to die and go we know not where;
    To lie in cold obstruction and to rot;
    This sensible warm motion to become

A kneaded clod; and the delighted spirit
To bathe in fiery floods, or to reside
In thrilling region of thick-ribbèd ice,
To be imprison'd in the viewless winds
And blown with restless violence round about
The pendant world; or to be worse than worst
Of those that, lawless and incertain, thought
Imagines howling. 'Tis too terrible!
The weariest and most loathèd worldly life
That age, ache, penury and imprisonment
Can lay on nature is a paradise
To what we fear of death.

HAMLET: To be or not to be, that is the question:
Whether 'tis nobler in the mind to suffer
The slings and arrows of outrageous fortune
Or to take arms against a sea of troubles
And by opposing, end them. To die, to sleep
No more, and by a sleep to say we end
The heartache and the thousand natural shocks
That flesh is heir to. 'Tis a consummation
Devoutly to be wish'd. To die, to sleep;
To sleep, perchance to dream—aye, there's the rub,
For in that sleep of death what dreams may come
When we have shuffled off this mortal coil,
Must give us pause. There's the respect
That makes calamity of so long life,
For who would bear the whips and scorns of time,
Th' oppressor's wrong, the proud man's contumely,
The pangs of dispriz'd love, the law's delay,
The insolence of office, and the spurns
That patient merit of th' unworthy takes
When he himself might his quietus make

With a bare bodkin? Who would fardels bear,
To grunt and sweat under a weary life,
But that the dread of something after death—
The undiscover'd country from whose bourne
No traveler returns—puzzles the will,
And rather makes us bear those ills we have
Than fly to others we know not of?
Thus conscience does make cowards of us all,
And thus the native hue of resolution
Is sicklied o'er with the pale cast of thought,
And enterprises of great pitch and moment
With this regard their currents turn awry
And lose the name of action.

Consider this question: in your desire to perform Shakespeare, have you allowed Isabella's voice (or Hamlet's or Juliet's) to speak for itself, or have you merely imposed your own?

If you're not sure, go back and start over. This time the same exercises will provide you with a different experience and new growth and understanding. As the Buddha says, "Everything changes; nothing remains without a change."

· 13 ·

The Ephemeral Nature of the Theatrical Event

THEATRE EXISTS only in that intangible moment when human beings share the same breath, within the same space, at the same moment, at the same event. This interaction, this communion, is delicate and transitory; it constantly comes to life and disappears. It is the fragile manifestation of that which can be expressed only at that particular moment, in that particular space, in that particular manner.

This process of manifestation is essentially ephemeral and unrepeatable, a fleeting moment in which something unique occurs, something which cannot be easily captured on film, video, or CD. The ephemeral in theatre cannot be discussed in analytic or therapeutic terms. Like true love, it makes no sense, is just as hard to find, and is priceless when you do find it.

Theatres themselves have always been homes to the ephemeral. Great theatres, such as the ancient Greek theatre at Epidaurus, the Comédie Française, the Berliner Ensemble, and Covent Garden are houses of shared secrets, where the ghosts of great performers walk the boards. There is a sense of myth and tradition in these great public structures that affects performer and spectator alike. Such spaces offer a rite of passage, the promise of transformation and transcendence. The reconstructed Globe seeks to be such a great public structure, playing a role in society similar to that of its namesake.

The best example of a shared myth that I have encountered in the theatre is at the Kabuki-za in Tokyo. There, at the moment when the lead actor strikes a classic pose before launching into a famous speech, fans in the audience shout out the names of the great Kabuki actors who have played the role in the past. The effect is part challenge, part cheer, part claque—as if "Burton! Olivier! Gielgud!" were shouted in the brief pause after "To be, or not to be . . ." The audience is an informed, enthusiastic participant in a long theatrical tradition.

In modern, technological, mass-produced theatre, audiences are no longer encouraged to think or participate. They are hardly even required to listen or watch; wireless mikes and hyperkinetic computerized lighting tell them what to feel and when.

I believe we must cultivate an audience that cherishes the ephemeral in the theatre just as it does a first kiss, a favorite sunset, or a last embrace.

Venue, Voice, and Time

What are the necessary elements of ephemeral theatre? There are three elements that constitute the essential *form* of the theatrical event and define its *content*: venue, voice, and time. All performance, and indeed, all teaching, is defined by and is subject to venue, voice, and time.

First, we manipulate the fixed nature of venue by means of voice and time. A venue is a fixed place for both gathering and welcoming. By using venue in this manner, I want to imply the duality of this space: a place with a myth of purpose, where both the event and the architecture surrounding the event share in the construction of its meaning. At the levels of both form and content, then, venue implies potential.

No event can take place without an address; but this "fixed" space can become an infinite variety of other spaces where our imaginary forces transport us from our everyday lives.

Next, we manipulate the human nature of voice by means of venue and time. There can be no theatrical event without voice. Voice is the uniquely human power of utterance, of making ourselves known and understood in the world.

Even dance and mime provide voice. Voice means not only sound; voice is any agency of expression of one's anger, love, or sorrow. Most important, voice means the right and the opportunity for that expression. And voice is heard only over time.

Finally, we manipulate the subjective nature of time by means of voice and venue. There can be no theatrical event without time. Time is a continuum in which events occur in an apparently irreversible manner. Time is the interval separating two points on that continuum—sunrise and sunset, birth and death. Time is the relationship of change to that continuum, a measurement of growth, decay, aging, or renewal. Each of us has his or her own, subjective clock, constantly evaluating and judging time, even as we measure it. We constantly "play back the tapes" to recall a time when we were happier, sadder, or stronger; and we "fast forward" to a more ideal or frightening future. Time, then, can be a measurement of nostalgia, dread, or hope.

In creating the theatrical event, one of the most difficult

tasks is to create a shared sense of time—time equally precious to performer and spectator; and to make this time, in this venue, with these voices, unique and memorable. Every device we use in the theatre is geared to the manipulation of time.

On Volume

If venue, voice, and time define the content of a performance, and define its form, what binds that content, that form together in a way that makes those elements understandable to an audience? For me, the answer is *volume*. Volume, as I employ it, is three-dimensional, architectural, and geometric— the capacity of a performance.

An actor on stage defines one side of a six-sided cube. His body forms one plane, and the floor, ceiling, back, and two side walls of the venue make up the other five planes. The actor moving across the stage continually redefines the dimensions of this cube and therefore its volume. The great French actor Jean-Louis Barrault called this cube "a block of frozen silence, full of potentialities."

Because the true nature of the theatrical event is ephemeral, mastery of this volume—filling it with the actor's presence using the tools of venue, voice, and time—is a fundamental challenge of performance. Unless actor and audience are enclosed within the same volume, no theatrical event, ephemeral or otherwise, can occur.

The process of filling this volume is the process of defining ourselves and our relationships through drama. It is what gives meaning to the "imitation of action." It returns us to the ritual origins of theatre, the ritual of communion and shared experience. We create this shared experience through a theatrical language of codes, images, symbols, and actions. Without this shared language there is no understanding; no understanding, no event.

Because we can no longer assume that a sense of commonality exists with, or among, the audience, the creation of this volume, a sense of shared space, is crucial when presenting a play in a fragmented society. We must begin to create a shared experience as soon as the audience enters the theatre, well before the first word is spoken.

Theatrical systems are "open," three-dimensional systems with many possibilities for creativity at any given moment. Literary and cinematic systems are "closed" and two-dimensional. Their meanings are fixed on paper or in the final print of a film.

Words function very differently in open, three-dimensional systems than they do in closed, two-dimensional ones. In two-dimensional models, words (what Freud called "word-presentations") serve to "dampen and mediate the affective and sensory aspects of language." In the three-dimensional, open model the use of language liberates and celebrates exactly those otherwise dangerous or threatening aspects. Put more simply, characters from Oedipus to Lear and Hedda Gabler behave on stage in ways people cannot in society. This can be life-affirming and life-changing for both performer and spectator.

Theatre can be successfully adapted to therapeutic, literary, or cinematic uses. These adaptations have enormous value for personal expression and healing; for the presentation of culture and ideas; and for the dissemination and documentation of live events to wider audiences. But these uses are not theatre. Instant Shakespeare requires nothing less than an investigation and an exploration of the nature of the seminal theatrical event itself—before its adaptation to any other use.

Perhaps no playwright suffers more from adaptations to other uses than Shakespeare. His plays have been turned into films and musicals; into posters and slogans for advertising; into school projects to prevent teen suicide. The Globe even has a project in which his plays are used as models for business leadership. But these adaptations are merely uses for the theatre, not theatre itself.

Shakespeare's plays are the prime example of the essentially ephemeral nature of the *theatrical* event. The plays were written for immediate performance in a temporary structure where dynamic language played upon the "imaginary forces" of the spectator. The only elements of production were those of venue, voice, and time; there were no elaborate sets, costumes, or special effects. Using these three fundamental elements, Shakespeare could turn a "Wooden O" into the vasty fields of France, the seacoast of Bohemia, or an entirely "brave new world."

The challenge we face when we produce Shakespeare's plays is to transport the richness of their meaning, their language, and their stories from the sixteenth century into the twenty-first in the most dynamic manner possible. His plays, despite all the footnotes, theories, and commentaries, are simple, direct, and immediate, and they should be perceived as such by audiences.

In this process, an important truth to remember is this: Always serve the integrity of the author while honoring the intelligence of the audience. Many times I've seen actors and actresses play whining Helenas, simpering Julias, and Romeos so thick that no woman would ever fall for them, in order to get an easy laugh from an audience.

The audience will respond to the respect you show them, even if it does not understand every word of the play. Never sacrifice your intelligence and integrity in order to say a line of Shakespeare. This is especially important for actresses playing Shakespeare's women. Often Gertrude and Ophelia, for example, are played as ignorant victims, tossed about by their neurotic son/lover. Don't they have lives, agendas, wants, needs, issues, and desires of their own? Is Desdemona another helpless victim, or does she really believe she can tame her husband as she would a hawk? Would a modern woman ever agree to Friar Laurence's plan to be entombed as Juliet does?

In short, never make a character dumber than you are! We must find the answers, motivations, and causes in Shakespeare that we can live with in the twenty-first century. And in that search for the truth that lies behind the "why, etc.?" we must always respect the intelligence of the actor, the audience, and the author.

How do you, then, make the conventions of classical drama acceptable and understandable to a modern audience? I'd like to approach this question by first examining the two principal traditions of acting and producing Shakespeare.

· 14 ·

Neo-Nominalism:
A Philosophy of
Training and Performance

IS THERE SUCH A THING as classical acting? In the twenty-first century should there be? You've probably seen announcements in newspapers and theatre magazines for courses (usually held in Britain during the summer) where "classical acting" is featured. These courses consist of speech, stage combat, and period movement classes along with some scene study. When you add up all these bits and pieces, you become "Shakespearean."

There are also announcements for workshops offering contemporary approaches to the classics, usually at American regional theatres attached to universities. Here the classics serve as springboards for the exploration of gender, race, and class—issues which may have nothing to do with what Shakespeare wrote.

These two camps represent the training approaches of the two principal acting traditions. In the first, an Anglo-centric approach, Shakespeare and Shakespeare's language are perceived as heightened and poetic—meant to be spoken artfully, if not beautifully. The style is primarily verbal. In the latter, postmodern approach, the language is deconstructed—broken apart from its meaning(s)—into a primarily visual style.

I want to examine the roots of these traditions, their cultural and aesthetic underpinnings, in order to demonstrate the contrasting basis of my own approach. To do this, I must take an excursion into philosophy.

Realism

"Realism," as a philosophical doctrine, assumes that universals exist outside the mind. (This should not be confused with the theatrical realism of Ibsen and Zola, which aimed for a realistic depiction of life on stage, without idealization or romanticization.) Realism means that "truth," "justice," "God," and "Shakespeare" are universals preexisting in an ideal state. It is then up to us to realize them, to give them concrete form.

Realists regard Shakespeare's plays as timeless classics. There is missionary faith here that anyone encountering these masterpieces will be transformed forever. Productions of Shakespeare's plays based upon this outlook possess a style that is best described as Edwardian rather than Elizabethan; a style reflective of a lost era in Britain which (if it ever really existed) exists today only in Merchant-Ivory films. This is the style of Laurence Olivier, John Gielgud, John Barton, Kenneth Branagh, and the BBC videos.

Realist style is essentially musical. The plays rely heavily upon the sound of the words and the depth of the passionate emotions they engender. Branagh, even at his most cinematic, falls within this realist category. No matter how skilled his camera work, his films are essentially recordings of verbal performances. They have more in common with the great performances captured on old LPs than with film versions of Shakespeare by Akira Kurosawa, Orson Welles, or Roman Polanski.

This tradition is tied irrevocably, if unconsciously, to British ideas of culture and class. In America our ambivalence toward this tradition has always been an indicator of our cultural insecurity. The following passages from two American classics, John Steinbeck's *Travels with Charley* and Mark Twain's *Huckleberry Finn*, will give you an idea of both the awe and the suspicion with which this tradition has been regarded by Americans. First, Steinbeck and his dog Charley when they encounter an itinerant actor:

"Tell me about your material. What do you use?"

He looked down at his hands and I saw that they were well-kept and very white, as though he wore gloves most of the time. "I hope you won't think I'm stealing material," he said. "I admire the delivery of Sir John Gielgud. I heard him do his monologue of Shakespeare— *The Ages of Man.* And then I bought a record of it to study. What he can do with words, with tones, and inflections!"

"You use that?"

"Yes, but I don't steal it. I tell about hearing Sir John, and what it did to me, and then I say I'm going to try and give an impression of how he did it."

"Clever."

"Well, it does help, because it gives authority to the performance, and Shakespeare doesn't need any billing, and that way I'm not stealing his material. It's like I'm celebrating him, which I do."

"I think Gielgud would be pleased."

"Oh! I wrote him and told him what I was doing and how I was doing it, a long letter." He brought out a lumpy wallet . . . and with careful fingers unfolded a small sheet of note paper with the name engraved at the top. The message was typed. It said, "Dear . . . : Thank you for your kind and interesting letter. I would not be an actor if I were not aware of the sincere flattery implied in your work. Good luck and God bless you. John Gielgud."

I sighed, and watched his reverent fingers fold the note . . . and put it away. "I never show that to anyone to get a show," he said. "I wouldn't think of doing that."

And I'm sure he wouldn't. . . .

. . . So it went on—a profession older than writing and one that will probably survive when the written word has disappeared. And all the sterile wonders of the movies and television and radio will fail to wipe it out—a living man in communication with a living audience. . . .

And now from *Huckleberry Finn*, a passage in which Huck describes his adventures on a Mississippi riverboat:

. . . After dinner the Duke says:

"Well, Capet, we'll want to make this a first-class show, you know, so I guess we'll add a little more to it. We want a little something to answer encores with, anyway."

"What's onkores, Bilgewater?"

The Duke told him, and then says:

"I'll answer by doing the Highland fling or the sailor's hornpipe; and you—well, let me see—oh, I've got it—you can do Hamlet's soliloquy."

"Hamlet's which?"

"Hamlet's soliloquy, you know; the most celebrated thing in Shakespeare. Ah, it's sublime, sublime! . . ."

. . . He told us to give attention. Then he strikes a most noble attitude, with one leg shoved forwards, and his arms stretched away up, and his head tilted back, looking up at the sky; and then he begins to rip and rave and grit his teeth; and after that, all through his speech, he howled, and spread around, and swelled up his chest, and just knocked the sports out of any acting ever I seen before. This is the speech—I learned it, easy enough, while he was learning it to the king:

To be, or not to be; that is the bare bodkin
That makes calamity of so long life;
For who would fardels bear, till Birnam Wood do
     come to Dunsinane,
But that the fear of something after death
Murders the innocent sleep,
Great nature's second course,
And makes us rather sling the arrows of outrageous
     fortune
Than fly to others we know not of.
That's the respect must give us pause:
Wake Duncan with thy knocking! I would thou
     couldst;
For who would bear the whips and scorns of time,
The oppressor's wrong, the proud man's contumely,
The law's delay, and the quietus which his pangs
     might take,
In the dead waste and the middle of the night, when
     churchyards yawn
In customary suits of solemn black,
But that the undiscovered country from whose bourne
     no traveller returns,

Breathes forth contagion on the world,
And thus the native hue of resolution, like the poor
    cat i'the adage
Is sicklied o'er with care,
And all the clouds that lowered o'er our housetops,
With this regard their currents turn awry,
And lose the name of action.
'Tis a consummation devoutly to be wished. But soft
    you, the fair Ophelia:
Ope not thy ponderous and marble jaws,
But get thee to a nunnery—go! . . .

Banging at swords!

Essentialism

Opposed to this tradition of realism, with its assumptions
about the beauty and universal meaning of Shakespearean
language and style, is the theory of an "essentialist" Shakespeare.

Essentialism holds that a being's ultimate reality, its
essence, lies only in what is perceptible to the senses. For example, the biblical story of "Doubting Thomas" is an essentialist view of faith. The apostle Thomas refused to believe in
Christ's Resurrection until he could "see with his own eyes
and touch with his own hands" the wounds suffered by Jesus
on the cross. He would believe only in a reality perceptible to
his senses. Just as the realist tradition of Shakespeare belongs
to great British actors like Gielgud and Olivier, the essentialist Shakespeare belongs to the modern European director of
"total theatre." Here, image, body language, and movement
take precedence over speech. In this kind of Shakespearean

production, concept and metaphor are often more important than the word.

The essentialist Shakespeare is physical and sensory; a Shakespeare of athletics, "empty spaces," and unifying images. It is the Shakespeare of directors like Orson Welles, Peter Brook, Ariadne Mnouchkine, Peter Stein, and others who have made Shakespeare our contemporary, with productions of Kabuki *Tempests,* Star Wars *Henrys*, Mafia *Much Ados*, and Wild West *Shrews*.

This essentialist Shakespeare is often political, with a Marxist or at least a populist bent. It is intent on liberating Shakespeare from the assumed tyranny of the British upper classes; freeing it, in other words, from the realist Shakespeareans.

It was argued, until recently, that this "rough" kind of theatre is the more culturally relevant and politically correct of the two schools of thought. But no longer. In recent years the advent of postmodernist readings and productions has changed all that.

Postmodern readings and productions of Shakespeare, heavily influenced by academic theory and literary criticism (deconstructionism, new historicism, feminism, etc.) replaced the central truths of the plays with marginal theorizing. The plays became, rather than self-contained dramatic events, "pretexts" for performances intended to explicate a prevailing theory. Shakespeare became secondary to Derrida, Freud, Lacan, Brecht, and Boal. Text and image were intentionally fragmented and became self-referential events to be observed. Interdependence of text and image was replaced by "interstitiality" between text and image, rendering the texts "open" and "fluid," as opposed to "closed" and "fixed." All options, all readings, all endings became equally valid.

Postmodern Shakespeare, then, is a vehicle for opinion. There is no "essence" in this new essentialism—texts are cut up beyond recognition, words repeated and rearranged, scenes replaced by images or sounds. What Shakespeare says about us matters less here than what we say about Shakespeare.

In the hands of gifted individuals like Robert Wilson (*King Lear*) or Heiner Müller (*Hamlet Machine*), Shakespeare can be the basis for brilliant new work in the theatre in much the same way that Verdi turned *Othello, Macbeth,* and *The Merry Wives of Windsor* into grand operas. But postmodern stagings of the plays are more often than not exercises in sterile semiotics and fashionable ironic attitudes. The result is not a vision of Shakespeare but simply a version of Shakespeare.

Directors in the sixties and seventies believed they were freeing the theatre from the tyrannies of the text and Anglo-centrism. They addressed what Peter Brook called "a hunger" in the theatre, a collective longing for a shared experience in which the audience was a central participant and not merely an optional observer. For all the mass of scholarship and critical writing behind today's postmodern performances, they do very little to satisfy our collective hunger for understanding or even for entertainment.

Is it possible to serve the integrity of the text in an era of cultural illiteracy; to honor the intelligence of an audience numbed by television and film? Can we find a theoretical foundation for a style which will satisfy this hunger as we begin the twenty-first century?

While searching for answers, I came upon a school of thought that provided the philosophical foundation I sought for my own work.

A New Nominalism

Nominalism, a theory that flourished in Europe between the eleventh and fourteen centuries, held that there are no universal essences in reality; that only individual, or particular cases of classification exist. In other words, it is not possible to talk or write about "animal," "man," "God," or "Shakespeare" in general. Such words, said the nominalists, were only *flatus vocis*, sounds without meaning.

This is where the nominalists got into trouble with the realists of the church. The realists said that from the acorn you could infer the existence of the oak tree that produced it, and the acorn that produced that, and so on, until you reached the first oak without an acorn, the prime mover unmoved, or God. "God," in his perfect form, was out there, waiting to be realized.

The nominalists disagreed. It is not possible, they believed, to connect this particular acorn to anything except my particular knowledge of it. This caused quite a theological row until William of Occam forged a great compromise. Occam, the originator of the maxim we call Occam's Razor—that "the simplest cut is closest to the truth"—said that articles of faith were based upon faith alone and not subject to principles of reason. Then there was peace in the church. Fascinating, I admit, but how does nominalism apply to Instant Shakespeare?

First, my neo-nominalism means that "Shakespeare," "tragedy," "comedy," "Hamlet," "Desdemona"—or their essential qualities—do not preexist in some pure state; that a real or essential Shakespeare cannot be inferred. If the words spoken on stage are to be more than just *flatus vocis*, their agreed-upon meaning must be made concrete *only* at the moment they come into existence.

Sound familiar? This is the basis of everything we did in Part One. My nominalism is the underpinning of the frog overlays, "this, not that," and "why, etc.?" It sustains my belief in the provisionality of meaning. When our work becomes generic, resting on assumptions about "Shakespeare," "Derrida," "culture," or "language," or, worse, issues of gender, race, and class, then at that moment meaning ceases to exist.

Let me put it another way. With all the new plays being written, films made, and CDs burned, why should we continue to read, produce, perform, and teach the four-hundred-year-old writings of a dead white Anglo-Saxon? Not because he is "the greatest playwright the English language ever produced" (maybe he is, maybe he isn't). Not because of his place in the canon of "culture" (maybe we should keep him, maybe we shouldn't). And not because we can produce his plays royalty-free and cast a lot of students in the school play. We read and perform Shakespeare because, at this particular moment, this play speaks to us as no other play can or will; because we have a hunger to create and share this particular event with other human beings.

The logical extension of neo-nominalism means no more Shakespeare required in the curriculum, no summer Shakespeare festivals, no Royal Shakespeare Company, no Ph.D. dissertations in Shakespeare. In short, no Shakespeare industry. Is that such a bad thing? Imagine how much bad Shakespeare could be eliminated if there were a fundamental requirement to actually say something urgent and immediate in the Shakespeare play you were presenting.

The audience that saw a play at the Globe in 1599 might have witnessed a bear-baiting earlier in the day, where dogs ripped out the ears and tongue of a bear and then brought the animal down. After the play they may have gone to a

Southwark brothel, or to see an execution at the Tower of London. There was nothing virtual, polite, or politically correct about Shakespeare's world. Certainly it is a good thing that we have come a long way since then in our standards of social justice. But if, like our counterparts in the eighteenth and nineteenth centuries, we believe that Shakespeare's plays are barbaric and outdated, we are under no compulsion to produce them. Shakespeare's plays are visceral, sexual, sensual experiences—they should grab you by the gut, shake you up, and not let you sleep for a week! Is this too much to ask of theatre in the twenty-first century?

· 15 ·

Presence and the Ontological Sensibility

THE EXERCISES throughout this book, from the frog overlays to the push-ups, comprise a histrionic grammar, a set of three-dimensional tools for plumbing the meanings in Shakespeare's texts. This process is primarily experiential: as the meanings in our work become clear, we take responsibility for the artistic decisions we make. By accepting this responsibility, we step into the light of what George Steiner in *Real Presences* (1989) calls "accountable presence."

Meaning, as I have hinted throughout, can be found only in the commitment to provisionality. What is in the sand today will not be in the sand tomorrow. We must act as if we were convinced of a text's absolute and final meaning, knowing that absolute finality is neither possible nor even desirable. For example, one of the first rules of Instant Shakespeare is to make the nouns sound like what they mean. But what does a noun actually "mean"? To quote Steiner at length:

> . . . The word *rose* has neither stem nor leaf nor thorn. It is neither pink nor red nor yellow. It exudes no odor. It is,

per se, a wholly arbitrary phonetic mark, an empty sign. Nothing whatever in its (minimal) sonority, in its graphical appearance, in its phonemic components . . . has any correspondence to what we believe or imagine to be the object of its purely conventional reference. Of that object "in itself," of its "true" existence or essence, we can . . . know strictly nothing . . . the word *rose* cannot instruct us. . . . To ascribe to words a correspondence to "things out there," to see and use them as somehow representational of "reality" in the world, is not only a vulgar illusion. It makes of language a lie. . . . The truth of the word is the absence of the world.

Substitute *dagger* for *rose* in the moment when Macbeth "sees" the dagger. At that moment there should be no doubt in Macbeth's mind, in the mind of the actor playing him, or in the mind of the audience about what the word "dagger" "means"—what it looks like, why he sees it, or what effect seeing it will have on him. This concordance between character, actor, and audience exists even if tomorrow night the same performed moment has a completely different set of meanings; even if the *word* "dagger" won't cut butter, let alone Duncan's throat! This commitment to the provisionality of the concordance that occurs in performance, the agreed-upon "as if" of meaning, shared by audience and performer, is the act of faith that makes presence possible.

Presence is the elusive ability of people, places, and things to imprint our lives and leave us transformed. In the "real world," presence resides in the realms of religion, music, love, and death. But what about on stage? If Aristotle, in *The Poetics*, is correct in saying that tragedy is an "imitation of an action," what kind of actions do we imitate in order to invoke presence?

Members of some fundamentalist and Pentecostal sects experience the presence of God when dancing, speaking in tongues, or laying on hands. In this experience is a sense of possession, of being taken over entirely by the "other." In this way the faithful, the chosen, and the converted come to know God; they are touched, redeemed, and made whole. The burning bush that spoke to Moses and the lightning bolt that knocked St. Paul off his horse were manifestations of divine presence—material signs interpreted by them to be God.

Moments of presence can also be felt in music, not only in the music of Mozart and Mahler but also in popular music. Humphrey Bogart thinks of Ingrid Bergman when Sam plays it again; Cole Porter gets you "under his skin," "night and day." Country and western music is full of empty pillows; and the blues got it bad and that ain't good. Music is like perfume: one whiff of the right scent and you're gone. Just a few bars and we are overwhelmed by the presence of "the other."

Presence is what you "feel across a crowded room" on some "enchanted evening": you meet a stranger, and before words are even spoken, you are overwhelmed by the being of another—a combination of grace, love, passion, and personality, summed up in just a few notes.

One of the most complete experiences of presence occurs when we are in love: we want to be with "the other" all the time. While you might use every one of the song lyrics above to describe your beloved, an encounter with presence most often takes place in silence: in the look, the touch, the embrace, or the kiss. We sense the presence of the loved one even when he or she is far away, or long gone. Author Milan Kundera, in *The Unbearable Lightness of Being*, calls this "the golden footprint": ". . . Sabina's physical presence was much less important to him than he had suspected. What was important was the golden footprint, the magic footprint she had left on his life and no one could ever remove. . . ."

An even greater experience of presence occurs when the loved one doesn't return our love; we become obsessed and possessed by what Roland Barthes calls nonpresence. We lose sleep over the loved one and long for him or her. We sit, pace, toss, and turn waiting for the phone to ring, the letter to arrive, the door to open. This is why love hurts.

Finally, Death, when the matter of the body becomes inanimate, is the ultimate test of presence. Beyond motion, what proof of actually having "lived" remains?

Hamlet is driven mad by the fact that his mother seems to carry no "footprint" of his father's presence. Hamlet fails to understand that the experience of presence in life is an intimate one—it occurs only between "one" and "another." His own experience of the presence of his father, whether ghost or a psychological manifestation, is unique to him and not graspable by anyone else. Even if the ghost's manifestations to Hamlet are observed by Gertrude, Polonius, and Ophelia, they can only speculate on their meaning.

Both *observation* and *speculation* define varieties of seeing. Observation is rooted in physics, speculation in metaphysics. We observe the burning bush, the stranger across a crowded room, or the ghost, but we speculate on its meaning. This difference between observation and speculation, between physics and metaphysics, defines the difference between performance and presence. You can observe a performance, but you can only speculate on the possibility of presence within that performance. Performance is the physical manifestation of interpretation, the *sine qua non* of presence, the condition without which presence (a metaphysical quality) is not possible in the theatre.

It is possible to read the history of drama, including the

Bible, as a history of the nearness of "the other," the proximity of presence. The Greeks, as well as the Old Testament prophets, believed that the gods took an active, sometimes vindictive role in their everyday lives. For the Elizabethans, presence, religious as well as royal, was a fact of daily life. Sir Thomas More went to the executioner's block comforted by his belief in divine presence; common folk lived convinced of the real presence of witches, ghosts, fairies, and goblins and their influence on their everyday lives.

Not until the Age of Enlightenment did drama begin to lose touch with presence and occupy itself with contemporary social and political issues. Today democracy has long since replaced the divine right of kings. Science, industry, technology, advertising, and consumerism have pushed us to a point where we rarely speak of our faith in presence.

Yet presence is the intangible, invisible element that can make a performance great and memorable. Moments of presence have such an impact on our real lives that it is obvious that re-creating them on stage is an essential element of good theatre.

Shouldn't we seek to create characters who will leave their "golden footprint" on us? If, as Ralph Harper writes, "presence lingers," shouldn't we try to create Ophelias, Cordelias, Hamlets, or Lears who linger long after the actual performance?

The Ontological Sensibility

Earlier I used Francis Fergusson's phrase "histrionic sensibility" to describe the ability to read a text in its three-dimensionality, the way a musician reads a score or an architect a blueprint. The study of presence in performance requires the development of what I call, with apologies to Fergusson, the *ontological sensibility*.

Ontology is the study of being. An actor on a stage exists on one level of being; the character that actor portrays is a second level; the author behind that character is a third.

The purpose of the ontological sensibility is to fill the play with beings who linger. That desire is essential even though, more often than not, we will fail in our efforts; a capacity for presence can be developed, but presence itself cannot be commanded, ordered up, or even taught. It can only be valued, invoked, and wished for.

The ontological sensibility presumes the existence of the histrionic sensibility. Presence cannot exist without a technically solid performance. Performance, even good performance, however, can exist without presence. Presence therefore presumes performance. But performance is ephemeral; presence lingers.

In the preceding chapter we discussed the ephemeral nature of the theatrical event; what happens in performance is fleeting and must be defined by its volume. Volume, you will remember, is defined as the capacity of a performance. If presence has the potential to transcend the ephemeral, to "stay with us" after the event, then presence is the lingering content of performance.

There is a "grammar" for the ontological sensibility just as there is one for the histrionic, even though following it brings no guarantee of success. Otherwise every performance would be radiant. Who would want it otherwise? All we can do is work hard and hope for the best. "Just do your work, then let go," the Master of the Tao wrote.

In order for presence to exist in performance, three prerequisite levels of presence must be fulfilled and three prerequisite conditions met.

Prerequisite Levels of Presence in Performance

The three prerequisite levels of presence are:

1. The presence of the self.
2. The presence of the character.
3. The presence of the author.

In Shakespeare the presence of the *self* is established through the monologue. Many of the verbal and physical exercises we performed in Part One are designed to lay the groundwork for the presentation of a unified, unbifurcated self in performance. To quote Steiner again:

> [In Shakespeare] one must be able to hear grammar made music. The issue is the rare participial boldness of Titania's "childing"; it is that of one's grasp of the wondrous aptness of Oberon's "throned *by* the west," where commonplace "throned *in*" would not do. The attempt must be made to elucidate grammatically "There sleeps Titania sometime of the night" so as to tease out something of an intelligible part—even the subtlest grammarian-listener can do no more—of its technical magic, of that which makes the footfall of meaning enigmatically lustrous as would no other syntactic turn or "deviance" from the eroded and expected in daily usage.

In short, the presence of the self becomes clear every time you decide why "this particular character says these particular words at this particular moment, in this particular order." You are present, having made a choice and taken responsibility for it.

The presence of the *character* is established through the choices made during the process of "this, not that" in the scene. Faced with moments of crisis and disequilibrium, characters define themselves through "character-in-action," through the confrontations with the "either/or" choice given to them. Lear and Cordelia's "nothing" dialogue is an example of this "either/or" confrontation. When asked to speak again, they can either say "nothing" or "something" at that moment; but what they choose to say defines who they are.

These moments of crisis and decision, of choosing "this, not that," are played in the "space between the lines" of a scene. They lead to a moment of "maximum disequilibrium," to use John Howard Lawson's phrase, when a boundary situation, such as Lear and Cordelia's, must be confronted.

Boundary situations, as the theologian Karl Jaspers called them, are those moments when profound emotions—love, death, guilt, and agony—challenge us most deeply; when we feel we might crack if we were to make the wrong decision. A great play and a great performance are made up of a series of escalating boundary situations in which a character is gradually reduced to his or her essence.

It is not Lear's raging on the heath that defines him but the moment when he and Cordelia finally "sing like birds in a cage." It is not Hamlet's melancholy that defines him but the ultimate acceptance he finds in the "special providence" in the fall of a sparrow. The process these characters endure may be tortuous and tempestuous, but the ultimate moment achieved is one of clarity, acceptance, tranquility, and peace.

In the confrontation with, and release from, these boundary situations, the characters achieve the potential for presence. In these moments, presence, if it is to appear, demands an "as if" response. Hamlet must act "as if" the readiness were all, Lear "as if" love weighs more than "nothing," and so on. If we do not ask our characters to act provisionally, to act "as if," Isabella could never kneel, Lear and Cordelia never reconcile, Hamlet never find peace, except for the fact that the playwright says they do!

This provisionality, this demand that we accept each moment on stage as inevitable without being obvious, is the only thing that keeps our classics from becoming clichés. Since we know the end of the play, why sit through it again? We engage in the theatrical event because it provides us with the opportunity to experience presence: to encounter a "golden footprint."

It is in the classics that the presence of the *author* needs to be made most clear, through careful pre-performance reading and detailed transmission of the text in performance. We may never know what Shakespeare "meant," but we must act, in every sense of the word, "as if" we did, otherwise we substitute opinion for meaning. In other words, we must not mistake the voice of the agent for that of the author.

And no authorial presence looms larger in the English-speaking theatre than Shakespeare's. He presides over every production, every lecture, every rehearsal, and every book (including this one). But rather than treating him as an icon, I've posed an alternative (if not heretical) way of looking at Shakespeare the author: that we don't talk about "Shakespeare" but rather about this line, this fragment, and this word. We derive our meaning, our events, and ultimately our respect for Shakespeare's creative force through a deep and genuine encounter with his work, not his image or his reputation.

The Princess's Golden Footprint

The "Marcade" scene in *Love's Labours Lost* is effective because, in just a few lines, we experience maximum presence: the presence of the actor playing Marcade, the presence of his character, even the presence of the King whom we never see. Most important, we experience all three prerequisite levels of presence in the actions of the Princess of France.

Even in this most frivolous of comedies, the Princess finds herself in a boundary situation: she is torn between her duty to her kingdom and her attraction to the young King of Navarre, who has just offered himself to her in marriage. In this moment she may transcend herself and achieve a level of presence we have not seen in her previously.

PRINCESS: . . . A time methinks too short
　　To make a world-without-end bargain in.
　　No, no, my lord, your grace is perjured much,
　　Full of dear guiltiness and therefore this:
　　If for my love (as there is no such cause)
　　You would do aught, this shall you do for me:
　　Your oath I will not trust, but go with speed
　　To some forlorn and naked hermitage,
　　Remote from all the pleasures of the world;
　　There stay until the twelve celestial signs
　　Have brought about their annual reckoning.
　　If this austere insociable life
　　Change not your offer made in heat of blood,
　　If frosts and fasts, hard lodging and thin weeds
　　Nip not the gaudy blossom of your love,
　　But that it bear this trial and last love
　　Then, at the expiration of the year,
　　Come challenge me, challenge me by these deserts,
　　And by this virgin palm now kissing thine,
　　I will be thine. . . .

The heart of the "being" that is comprised of the actress, the Princess, and Shakespeare must be ready to break at the boundary moment when the young King of Navarre offers her his hand in marriage and she chooses to turn him down.

Prerequisite Conditions of Presence in Performance

The three prerequisite conditions necessary for presence to occur in performance are:

1. The text must be significant.
2. The characters must be touched.
3. The actor must be available.

Significance implies import, consequence, and expressiveness. We create because we believe we have something significant to say at a particular moment, in a particular place, in a particular manner. If we act "as if" that is the case, then we may occasionally achieve presence in our work.

Significance is not presumed simply because of the playwright's or director's or actor's biography. Shakespeare's texts are neither more nor less significant than any others in regard to their presumption of presence. A child's grade-school pageant may have as much, if not more, potential for presence as a routine production of "a classic." The key issue is whether you, the character, and the playwright are actually "there," present with the audience at the ephemeral moment of the theatrical event, trying to make contact, to be understood, to linger.

In order for the text to achieve significance, the characters must be *touched*, in every sense of the word: they must be a little mad and a little moved; they must be "touchable" in the tactile sense—hence my emphasis on three-dimensionality, texture, and "tune."

Characters touched in this way find themselves in boundary situations where they are aliens, unable to accept or tolerate realities that seem benign to everyone around them. Think of Hamlet in the first court scene: "Seems, Madame? I know not seems." He cannot tolerate hypocrisy.

This disequilibrium leads to nostalgia, a "looking for the lost," as the journalist Alan Booth put it. *Hamlet*, for example, is about a search for lost presences on many levels—the ghost, the lost love of Gertrude and Ophelia, Hamlet's own lost self.

Hamlet holds himself up to "reflection" which, like observation and speculation, is another form of seeing. He compares himself to a player who can weep for Hecuba and to twenty thousand men who go to their graves as if they were beds. Looming over him are the "presences" of his father, Claudius, and Fortinbras, a leader who seems to possess all the princely qualities that Hamlet fears he himself lacks. Hamlet must, in a pattern that recurs in Shakespeare, flee his home in order to return and claim himself—"'Tis I! Hamlet, the Dane."

There are many homeless and dispossessed characters in Shakespeare. Lear on the heath and Rosalind in the forest are strangers in a strange land. Othello and Desdemona are both uprooted—he from the battlefield, she from Venice—a sure formula for disaster. How often are Shakespeare's characters "tossed about" by storms and tempests? Not only the shipwrecked Hamlet but Lear, Prospero, Viola, and Pericles find themselves in the "sunshine after storm" (the title of one Japanese translation of *The Tempest*).

Shakespeare was a master at creating boundary situations from which his characters were forced to escape. This moment of escape is one of the things Aristotle meant by "recognition" on stage. We and the character on stage become aware that something which has been dislocated is now, literally, "put back into place." And we—all of the "we's" contained in the cycle of performance—feel ourselves whole and complete again.

One of the great boundary situations in Shakespeare occurs at the end of *Macbeth*. Birnam Wood has marched, Macduff is of no woman born, and Macbeth, a lying, murdering villain for most of the play, faces his comeuppance. In a good performance, when Macbeth refuses escape and throws his shield before his body, we feel the shiver of recognition and awareness go through the actor and the audience as Macbeth becomes himself again. We root for this completion, for the return of his lost honorable self. It is as close as we come to redemption in the theatre.

It is the "essence of tragedy," as Maxwell Anderson called it, that these recognition scenes come too late. We feel the tragic loss of what might have been if Macbeth, Hamlet, or Lear had come to themselves sooner.

In the creation of characters like Hamlet and Desdemona, presence does not come easily. The actor or actress playing these roles must be psychologically and emotionally *available* throughout the entire journey created for the character by the playwright.

To be available one must be open, vulnerable, honest, and prepared. In *On Presence*, one of the definitions Ralph Harper gives for presence is "the ability to make promises and to keep them," to show up. Isn't that what we do in bringing a text to life? We make a promise to give it voice, to struggle through rehearsals, and to show up—the character and the author with us—on opening night.

Availability in the actor is the capacity to imagine lives other than our own and to present them fully and honestly in performance. Availability requires modesty. If we are too full of ourselves, or worse, too afraid of ourselves, there is no room for "the other" to live within us. Performance is one of the rare opportunities we have in modern life to make presence possible, to make "the invisible visible."

Martin Buber, the "I/Thou" theologian, wrote that presence occurs in "strange, lyric, dramatic episodes, seductive, magical, [which] tear us away to dangerous extremes, shattering our security." Doesn't that sound like a good description of a theatrical event? Don't you want your acting and directing to achieve those strange, lyric, and dramatic moments? Don't you want to shatter the security of your audiences? Don't you want your presence, and that of the character you portray and the author you represent, to linger with the audience long after it has gone home?

The Histrionics of Presence

When the ephemeral elements of venue, voice, and time have slipped away, what remains is the imprint of the event. This experience of presence is rich and complex; it demands in turn a subtle response. Presence is not acknowledged in standing ovations or rave reviews but rather in what Coleridge called "the deep stillness" in which "truth can be apprehended," or, as Barrault wrote, "the Silence upon which life reposes."

Presence cannot be judged or evaluated. Presence is experienced; we cannot say that someone else's God, music, lover, or theatrical event is better than our own.

There is no virtual presence. Presence exists as surely as you do as you read this book. Presence demands technical elegance, what Hemingway meant when he talked about grace under pressure. How can you be available to give Isabella "voice" if you're stumbling over her lines, struggling with her costume, or unsure of her motivation?

Presence will not be commanded. It comes with hard work and faith—faith that what you say and how you say it are significant; that even in failure you have done your best. One of the most frustrating things in the theatre is to experience presence in rehearsal one night and then never see it again; to know it was there and be unable to re-create it. Availability has no short cuts.

Your risk as an actor is that you may never have the opportunity to perform a "significant" text or a "touched" character. When the opportunity arrives after years of struggle, there may be little of your own presence still "available." Not only do the trappings of fame and fortune dull us to the intimate encounters of presence in our lives, but we also learn a fatal lesson: we learn to act. Worse, we learn to pretend to be present.

Technique in the absence of presence is the province of the performing seal or prostitute. If you have nothing to say in which you have an urgent personal investment, your performance will lack authenticity and integrity. Presence in performance resonates with the audience only when the actor stands with his or her character and faces the abyss of conditionality, the abyss of "as if." As Isabella tells us, we must "knock there" and pose the terrifying questions of who we are and what we are capable of.

Epilogue:
Still Banging at Swords—
Optional Authenticity and
Shakespeare's Globe,
1997–2001

IN ONE OF MY FAVORITE PHOTOS of Sam Wanamaker, he is slightly unshaven, wears a casual plaid shirt, and has his arms wrapped around a nineteenth-century bust of a smiling Shakespeare. I can envision Sam digging this bust out of his attic and bringing it to the experts at *Antiques Roadshow*. Shakespeare was his prized possession, and Sam wanted everyone to value it as highly as he did.

Sam's obsession with Shakespeare began when he was a teenager living in a poor Jewish neighborhood in Chicago. He had his first taste of the plays at the Century of Progress, the world's fair held in Chicago in 1933. There the British pavilion included a replica of the Globe Theatre in which hour-long versions of several of Shakespeare's plays were presented. Umberto Eco, the noted cultural historian and author of *The Name of the Rose*, makes this point about fairs and expositions: "The basic ideology of an exposition is that . . . the building and the objects in it should communicate the value of a culture, the image of a civilization." Perhaps this explains why, in 1933, at an exposition celebrating progress, Britain was represented by a sixteenth-century playwright. Shakespeare expressed the "value of a culture," and Sam, ever the romantic, wanted to be a part of that culture. He fell in love with the image of Shakespeare as a marker of art and civilization.

His romance with Shakespeare continued into the late 1940s when, as a successful actor, he chose to stay in England rather than return to America and risk a subpoena to appear before the House Un-American Activities Committee. One day he decided to seek out the site of Shakespeare's theatre in south London. After much searching, he found only a plaque on a brewery wall marking the theatre that had once housed England's greatest playwright. (Today this wall fences off luxury condominiums from hordes of tourists.)

Sam was certain that this slight to Shakespeare should be corrected, and that he was just the man to do it. And, in fact, by the late 1960s he had convinced enough people of the value of his vision that a manifesto was drafted calling for a major redevelopment project in Southwark, one of London's poorest boroughs. Sam's "impossible dream" included offices, a library and museum, rehearsal space, a pub, and a replica—not a reconstruction—of the first Globe Theatre. There was even talk of putting a retractable plastic roof over the theatre. There certainly was no intention (as there was later on) of building the roof with thatch.

In 1971, scholars attending the First International Shakespeare Congress, held in Vancouver, Canada, gave their influential endorsement to Sam's now much-revised plan. Other than expressing the fear that it might become a Shakespeare Disneyland, no one mounted serious objections to the project. No one seriously believed the project would ever become a reality, but Sam used this validation from the academic community as a key component of his fund-raising efforts. Authenticity now became a matter of great importance. The Globe would be a faithful *reconstruction* of Shakespeare's theatre.

But which Globe would be built? The original of 1599 or the second Globe of 1614, built with a tile roof after the first theatre burned down? How many sides would it have? How many doors would be on the stage? Would they open in or out? Apart from a few modest summer Shakespeare productions under a leaky tent on Bankside, little else other than these debates and discussions was carried on until 1981. Then, in a surprise move, the same International Congress that had endorsed the project ten years earlier now refused to reendorse the new plan. Sam was outraged and responded by forming the International Shakespeare Globe Centre Trust. Under the auspices of the Trust, he brought together the key individuals who would eventually build the Globe—architect Theo Crosby, scholar Andrew Gurr, and industrialist Sir David Orr.

Only then, nearly thirty years after his first visit to Southwark's streets, did Sam's dream finally take on the prospect of realization. For the next fifteen years "authenticity" was the clarion call that rallied scholars, builders, and donors to the cause. The mission of the Globe became the "reconstruction of his [Shakespeare's] Globe Playhouse near its original Bankside site, as part of an international resource centre for people everywhere."

The authenticity debates touched upon everything from the size and shape of the theatre (eighty feet across? one hun-

dred? round? twenty-sided?) to the style of the interior and
the placement of the pillars. Even the position of the stage
within the theatre was an issue. Initially placed to catch most
of the afternoon sun, it was later decided that the stage
should be placed on a north/south axis. (This would allow an
even, shaded light to fall upon the actors and keep direct sun-
light out of their eyes.) The task of reconstruction was
further complicated by the usual modern architectural re-
quirements for handicap access, public restrooms, fireproof-
ing, and crowd control. Each point was settled only by long
discussion, debate, and, ultimately, compromise.

Still, in 1989, when the foundations of the nearby Rose
Theatre were discovered (and again in 1991, when parts of
the foundation of the Globe itself were found), arguments
were made that the new Globe, as designed, was too large—
that the relationship of architecture, actor, and audience
would not be accurate. This threatened to undermine the ra-
tionale upon which the decade-long fund-raising campaign
had been based. Sam and his team had succeeded in convinc-
ing donors (if not all scholars and theatre professionals) that
only a faithful reconstruction of the Globe near its original
site would produce new insights into Shakespeare's plays. An
authentic theatre, it was argued, would have an enormous
impact on the teaching and producing of Shakespeare world-
wide.

One of the more intriguing arguments against the size of
the Globe was offered by the historian Joy Hancox. Basing
her opinion on the Byrom Templates (sixteenth-century
drawings which match architectural designs for Roman theatres), she charged that "the structure is too big and out of
proportion with itself." This, she claimed, was because the
Byrom designs were based upon the mathematical laws of
proportion, which in Shakespeare's time were believed to un-

derpin the structure of the universe. The harmony in the design of the theatre reflected that of the cosmos and added another layer of meaning to the name chosen for the theatre. The word "globe" had entered the language only fifty years before. But as interesting as Hancox's theories were, by 1992 they were moot. The financial and intellectual investment made in building this particular Globe was too great, and construction went forward.

In the face of engineering realities and commercial considerations, more compromises with "authenticity" were made as the project proceeded. Thatch was weatherproofed. Stadium lights were added to make evening performances possible. The capacity of the pit, the size of the benches, and the height of the doors were adapted for modern, larger, spectators. And still no one seemed to know where the pillars should go! Authenticity was now becoming uncomfortably optional.

Gradually the claim to authenticity was transferred from the architecture of the building to the theatrical event it would house. It was now argued that the unique relationship of actor, audience, and architecture within the Globe would create an authentic playgoing experience in a theatre that Shakespeare himself would feel comfortable working in. But would it?

Shakespeare's plays, unlike those of Molière, Chekhov, Brecht, or the great Kabuki playwright Chikamatsu, had survived for more than four centuries without the benefit of a theatre dedicated to his legacy. There is no English theatre analogous to the Comédie Française, Moscow Art Theater, Berliner Ensemble, or Kabuki-za where traditions of Shakespeare performance have been handed down over time. In the years immediately following his death, Shakespeare's plays were performed by actors who may have been part of the Globe company, throughout the English countryside and in Europe, most notably in Germany. And soon thereafter, as English soldiers, sailors, and merchants began to cover and conquer the world, his plays were performed as far away as Africa and Asia. A line of actors passing down insights into Shakespearean roles can be traced to the reopening of the English theatres under Charles II, but by then any claims to authenticity were decidedly questionable, as tastes in plays and performers had changed.

The theatre of the Restoration, influenced by the French court where Charles spent his years in exile, regarded itself as more refined and sophisticated than the rough-and-tumble theatre of the Elizabethans and Jacobeans. By the eighteenth century, Shakespeare's plays were frequently revised to respond to the more "sensitive" tastes of the age. Lear and Cordelia, for example, reconciled and lived happily ever after in Colley Cibber's version of *King Lear*; and *All for Love*, John Dryden's adaptation of *Antony and Cleopatra*, was much preferred to the original. In the nineteenth century, Shakespeare's plays were cut and pasted to suit the talents of the great actor-managers of the day—Kean, Kemball, Macready, and Beerbohm-Tree. Not until the early twentieth century, in the work of William Poel and, later, Harley Granville-Barker, did authenticity become a value in Shakespeare performance. The Shakespeare tradition of the twentieth century owed far more to these Edwardians than it did to the Elizabethans.

Is it possible, then, in the twenty-first century, to create an authentic Elizabethan theatrical event? Is it even desirable?

The Globe's 2001 season brochure says that the acting company is composed not of "synthetic Elizabethans, but modern Elizabethans." I am not sure what a "synthetic" or a "modern" Elizabethan is. Surely the Globe is not advocating a return to Ye Olde Renaissance Fayre as it develops (as the brochure states) "new crafts in acting, dancing, costuming, and live music." I think, rather, it aspires to recapture an Elizabethan sense of exploration and creativity. Is this possible in our era? The Elizabethans, like most early modern Europeans, possessed two important characteristics that we do not.

Elizabethans were both metaphysical and linguistic. They believed in a spirit world—in the reality of heaven and hell and a life after death—and in the pantheistic world of the fairies and witches that populate Shakespeare's plays. To an Elizabethan, Queen Mab, Puck, and the Weird Sisters could actually exist. And the Elizabethans were obsessed with language, not merely with making puns and forming rhymes but with the concrete social value of words—oaths, curses, vows, proclamations, edicts, and banns. Their words carried much more weight than ours do today.

Today we are primarily literal and visual. Ours is the world of the atom, the genome, the pixel, the digit, the shot, the frame, and the sound bite. The Elizabethans could hear a play or a court case and retain much of it in memory. We, in turn, can watch the year's news highlights on television in sixty seconds on New Year's Eve and identify every split-second shot—and where we were when we first saw it!

In *Instant Shakespeare* we have spent a great deal of time getting our modern sensibilities around a phrase like Juliet's "Gallop apace, you fiery-footed steeds / Towards Phoebus' lodging . . . ," not because the vocabulary per se is alien to us but because the sensibility it expresses—one which sees the world in metaphor and frames it poetically—is. Yet, in spite of this vast difference between the sixteenth and twenty-first centuries, in its first four seasons the Globe mounted several "authentic" Shakespearean productions. It was their intention in each instance to give audiences as genuine an Elizabethan playgoing experience as possible.

The results were less than successful—a disappointing mixture of meticulously researched detail and inexplicable artistic license coexisting within the same productions. Authenticity became entirely optional—a vague and flexible standard, inconsistently applied.

Unfortunately, with the authority of its research, craftsmanship, and privileged position near Shakespeare's original theatre, the Globe, whether intentionally or not, misled audiences, teachers, and students of Shakespeare into believing that what they saw on stage was what Shakespeare intended. This is what I call the Vaticanization of the Globe—the suggestion of the infallibility of its artistic judgments based upon the weight of its architecture and its sacrosanct location. What saddens me more is that in the pursuit of this optional authenticity, the Globe has squandered an opportunity to create true theatrical events which engage and enlighten audiences. Fortunately, in its 2001 season, no "authentic" productions were scheduled—a sign, I hope, of a growing recognition of the theatre's potential. The reconstructed Globe is, whether historically accurate or not, a remarkable space for a theatrical encounter. It contains great possibilities for presence—actor and audience contained in the same volume, sharing the same event at the same time. It has yet to happen.

One of the most important lessons I hope you will take away from *Instant Shakespeare* is that there are no experts in Shakespeare. Each of us, if we read intelligently and without fear, has the right to our own Shakespeare, whether we love him, loathe him, are bored by his plays, or believe them to be the most compelling expressions of genius ever written. There is no authority that can place the seal of authenticity on Shakespeare. Each of the many institutions and individuals—myself included—who produce, edit, and play Shakespeare offers only an interpretation of a constantly challenging and changing text.

As I mentioned in the Introduction, I put off directing Shakespeare for a long time. When I was in junior high school, I was taken to see a production of *A Midsummer Night's Dream*. I remember nothing about it except that the actors spoke with forced British accents. The production was nothing more than "banging at swords." My grandparents spoke with Italian accents, and they were laughed at because of them. Were these British accents somehow better?

Later my high school drama teacher took our class to see Olivier's film version of *Othello*. I realize that it is the record of a landmark production, but at that time I couldn't keep from laughing. Here was an actor in black face rolling his eyes and banging at swords in the same movie theatre where I had seen stunning films by Fellini and Bergman. What planet were these Shakespeareans on? Didn't they know what twentieth-century acting was? But this was "Shakespeare"! It was "Olivier"! These words were spoken with great reverence. And who was I? At our house we still had plastic slipcovers on our furniture.

Those were my first, unfortunate encounters with Shakespeare. My later encounters have been, in many respects, happy accidents that have allowed me to be present at the creation of the new Globe. I hope my journey has been an authentic one, and I hope my authenticity has never been optional. I have endeavored to make every word, line, action, and production true in that particular moment. I may not always have succeeded, but, as I have pointed out here, success is not always an accurate barometer of authenticity.

Why does this particular character say these particular words, in this particular order, at this particular moment? I don't know, but together we can search for the answers.

Acknowledgments

Thanks to Hugh and Velma Richmond, Charles Duff, Johanna Schmitz, Neville Shulman, O.B.E., and Elaine Turner for encouraging me to get things down on paper. Thanks to Ann and Trevor Dannatt, Kelli Elmer, and Mike Masone for providing me with rooms with views in London in which to write. Thanks to Jack Newell at Deep Springs College and Janet Headley at Loyola College in Maryland for visiting appointments that allowed me time to reflect and rewrite. Thanks to Diana Sherwood and Rabbi Clifford Librach for their insights into presence in and out of performance. Thanks to Cecelia Lopez, Margaret Stanek Fiore, Jennie Webb, Steven Memel, and Jill Holden, among many others, for reading and commenting upon various drafts. Thanks to Brad Berens at the University of California at Berkeley for the Coleridge reference. And thanks to Joyce Halsey for encouraging me to the end. To Mom and Dad, and Ray and Shirley, thanks for your support over twenty years of too much traveling.

Most of all, thanks to my students and colleagues in workshops and productions around the globe who suffered through push-ups and all the rest in the face of banging swords! They are the ones who have made *Instant Shakespeare* worthwhile.

A Note on Sources

The hundreds of books on Shakespeare range from the most scholarly and arcane to those about Shakespeare on cats and golf. There are dozens of editions of the plays and hundreds of books providing approaches to performing them. Something can be gleaned from all of them; much can be ignored in most of them.

I find three small books especially useful: E. M. W. Tillyard's *The Elizabethan World Picture* (London, 1944); Peter Brook's *The Empty Space* (New York, 1978); and Joseph Papp and Elizabeth Kirkland's *Shakespeare Alive!* (New York, 1988).

Gary Taylor's *Reinventing Shakespeare* (New York, 1991) gives a useful overview of the canonization of Shakespeare. Bertram Joseph's *Acting Shakespeare* (New York, 1969), while heavy going at times, is still the best book on Shakespeare's rhetoric and grammar. Obviously I think Francis Fergusson's *The Idea of a Theater* (Princeton, 1949) worth rereading, as is Aristotle's *Poetics*. Finally, although nearly a century old, Harley Granville-Barker's *Prefaces to Shakespeare* (London, 1993) still has much to offer.

These are basic books containing nuts-and-bolts insights into Shakespeare. They should be read before proceeding to more specialized, contemporary critics such as Stephen Greenblatt, Harold Bloom, Samuel Schoenbaum, Lisa Jardine, and Camille Paglia.

Of editions of Shakespeare's plays, I prefer the Arden editions of individual plays. Though there are sometimes more footnotes than text on a given page, you have in one edition most of the information you need to make a textual decision. For exactly the same reason, the Arden editions are difficult to act from. In production it is best to have available as many different editions of a play as possible. The selection process forces you to decide exactly what you want to say in each moment. I usually use the Folger texts to make my director's book—the text is printed on only one side, and the notes are largely irrelevant. I don't care for the Pelican editions; even though the notes have been moved from the back of the book to the bottom of the page, the texts are still too heavily punctuated for my taste.

I avoid "complete works," as most of them are not complete at all. Their heft alone gives the impression that Shakespeare's plays are, like the Bible, more to be respected than read. I would certainly avoid the new Oxford/Norton and Arden editions. The Arden has eliminated most of its useful notes, and the Oxford/Norton contains readings that are simply perverse (although many of the introductory essays are quite good). If you must have a complete set of the plays, the old Riverside and the relatively new Addison Wesley editions are as good as any. A facsimile edition of the First Folio, from either Norton (currently out of print) or Folger, is also a useful reference.

My sources on theatre theory and criticism include Aristotle, *On Poetry and Style*; Antonin Artaud, *The Theatre and Its Double* (New York, 1958); Jean-Louis Barrault, *Reflections on the Theatre* (London, 1951); Hubert Witt, ed.,

Brecht: As They Knew Him (New York, 1974); John Willet, ed., *Brecht on Theatre* (New York, 1994); Noel Coward, *Private Lives* (London, 1979); James C. Bulman, ed., *Shakespeare: Theory and Performance* (London, 1996); Uta Hagen, *Respect for Acting* (New York, 1973); John Howard Lawson, *The Theory and Technique of Playwrighting and Screenwriting* (New York, 1936); David Mamet, *On Directing Film* (New York, 1991); Plutarch, *Lives of the Romans*; and Kaja Silverman, *The Subject of Semiotics* (New York, 1983).

For further information on Shakespeare's Globe, I recommend Barry Day, *This Wooden O* (New York, 1998); Joy Hancox, *The Byrom Collection and the Globe Theatre Mystery* (London, 1992); and John Orrell and Andrew Gurr, *Rebuilding Shakespeare's Globe* (New York, 1989). The video *Shakespeare's Globe Theatre Restored* (TMW Media Group, 1997) documents the history of the new Globe and the workshop production of *Much Ado About Nothing* that I staged there.

Helpful texts on the subjects of presence and meaning include Nancy Amphoux, *Confessions of a Zen Nun* (New York, 1986); Ernest Becker, *The Denial of Death* (New York, 1973); Umberto Eco, *Travels in Hyperreality* (New York, 1986); Ralph Harper, *On Presence* (Philadelphia, 1991); George Steiner, *Real Presences* (Chicago, 1989); Martin Buber, *I and Thou* (New York, 1974); Karl Jaspers, *Basic Philosophical Writings* (Columbus, Ohio, 1986); and Lao-tzu, *The Book of the Way* (London, 1988).

General literary sources include Guy de Maupassant, *Selected Short Stories* (London, 1995); Milan Kundera, *The Unbearable Lightness of Being* (New York, 1984); John Steinbeck, *Travels with Charley in Search of America* (New York, 1962); Mark Twain, *The Adventures of Huckleberry*

Finn (1884); Samuel Coleridge, *The Plays of William Shake-speare* (1765); Robert Burton, *Anatomy of Melancholy* (1621); and Timothy Bright, *Treatise on Melancholy* (1586).

But not everything is gleaned from books. As I mentioned in my Introduction, it is through our encounters with others that we gain knowledge, skill, and an understanding of presence. With regard to Shakespeare in my life, Sam Wanamaker had the greatest impact, but I have been fortunate to study and work with significant teachers and directors. These include directors Alan Schneider, Mel Shapiro, Donn Murphy, and Karl Weber; filmmakers Jan Kadar and Alexander Mackendrick; and acting teachers Robert Benedetti and Nina Foch. The late W. Duncan Ross was also an important influence, as was Nancy Amphoux, who taught my Strasbourg students to love Shakespeare even when I couldn't. The golden footprints of these remarkable individuals have indelibly marked my path in Shakespeare.

Index

A NOTE ON THE AUTHOR

Louis Fantasia is director of the Teaching Shakespeare Through Performance Institute of the Shakespeare Globe Centre U.S.A. Born in Cambridge, Massachusetts, he studied at Georgetown University, the California Institute of the Arts, the American Film Institute Center for Advanced Film Studies, and the New York University School of the Arts. He has taught at the University of Southern California, the London Theatre School, Schiller College–Europe University, Deep Springs College, the Juilliard School, and Loyola College in Maryland, and has directed plays at international festivals as well as theatres in England, Europe, Japan, Australia, and the United States. From 1981 to 1991 he was director of Shakespeare Today, the Globe's acting and directing workshop. He lives in Los Angeles.